CIVIL JUSTICE AND THE POOR

CIVIL JUSTICE
AND THE POOR

Issues for Sociological Research

•

JEROME E. CARLIN
Coordinator, San Francisco Neighborhood
Legal Assistance Foundation

JAN HOWARD

SHELDON L. MESSINGER
Center for the Study of Law and Society
University of California, Berkeley

•

RUSSELL SAGE FOUNDATION
NEW YORK, 1967

Russell Sage Foundation was established in 1907 by Mrs. Russell Sage for the improvement of social and living conditions in the United States. In carrying out its purpose the Foundation conducts research under the direction of members of the staff or in close collaboration with other institutions, and supports programs designed to improve the utilization of social science knowledge. As an integral part of its operations, the Foundation from time to time publishes books or pamphlets resulting from these activities. Publication under the imprint of the Foundation does not necessarily imply agreement by the Foundation, its Trustees, or its staff with the interpretations or conclusions of the authors.

CONTENTS

FOREWORD

THE POVERTY PROGRAM and the legal issues it radiates, to which this Carlin, Howard, Messinger volume is addressed, may be traced to many sources — to origins in the values of Western civilization; to the social psychology of the times; and, of course, to the immediate exigencies of politics.

For lawyers, however, there is a pretty clear genesis in the great civil rights decisions of the Supreme Court of the United States. *Brown v. Board of Education*, and other decisions out of the same mold which firmly declare that all Americans without regard to race are equal, had two big side effects:

(1) The equal protection notion stimulated legal decisions that men must be treated equally by the law without regard to whether they are rich or poor. And so, there have been holdings that a defendant is entitled to a lawyer, and to a transcript, and otherwise to defend himself in criminal proceedings even though he cannot afford them. This line has barely begun and promises to carry over into issues like the right to bail, to engage a psychiatrist, to employ investigators, and so forth.

On the civil side, courts have held the poll tax unconstitutional as an impediment to voting by poor people. It is illegal to close the public schools in one county while keeping them open in another: this invidious denial is against the community generally, not merely Negroes. How far this development will continue is not yet clear. Already some of us are alleging that the constitution is violated when certain areas of a town are denied municipal services such as sewers, police protection, paving of the streets, recreational facilities, lighting, and so forth, when these are furnished to other sections. When all the swimming pools are in the part of town that needs public recreation least, and the poor parts of a city can't even turn on fire hydrants, that may not merely be unfair. It is quite possibly unconstitutional. If we develop a legal remedy on this issue alone, it will be much better than the trial by battle which brought portable swimming pools to some parts of Chicago in the summer of 1967. If the doctrine that municipal services must be furnished to rich and poor areas alike is valid, it is valid without regard to race — it is for all the poor.

(2) By far the greater contribution of the civil rights decisions, and acts of Congress inspired by those decisions, has been the awakening of conscience, the creation of crises, the confrontation with the ultimate reality that enforcement of the equal protection clause has required.

For generations racial segregation obscured issues of poverty while in its own manner generating a good deal of it. As long as Negroes could be kept behind the curtain, literally and figuratively (How many remember that in the 1950's Negroes traveling on railroad diners were physically seated behind a curtain!), the country could ignore their schooling, their economic status, their housing.

But once the decisions of the Court said that in principle all persons, without regard to race, must be treated as part of this country, that Negro school children may not be kept in segregated schools, awesome implications appeared. The Negro kid who was admitted to a white school didn't come from a decent colored school, much less a desegregated one. He most likely came from a home lacking much of the background that helps a child succeed in school. He came, probably, from an unlivable slum. He possibly had no father at home and his mother, or father, if he had one, couldn't get a decent job. Maybe he or she was unable to get work because of race. Just as likely he or she had no training to do a job under the new regime of automation and mechanization—even if a job could have been had.

In short, problems of society generally began to emerge. And they are not problems of race alone, but of poverty.

The two greatest spurs to improving American education since World War II, if we take education for an example, have been the launching of the Russian Sputnik and the school segregation cases. From those influences flowed institutions like Project Headstart and experiments in team teaching, teaching machines, educational parks, and other innovations.

The rethinking about schools is but an example of rethinking about the economy, about housing, about welfare programs, and the rights of other minorities that would not have occurred without the civil rights revolution. In a certain sense, if we ever find any satisfaction in the legacy of slavery, it is that it generated enough emotion and political force that certain issues confronting society generally now receive attention. Without the civil rights revolution no one can doubt that there would be no poverty program today.

Those of us who years ago were concerned solely with what I might call orthodox issues of civil rights have, little by little and for a time not fully realizing it, been dealing more and more with questions of poverty and issues that affect all Americans. Some of us have become involved in cases seeking to make precedent on poverty law questions similar to the way in which we have, over the years, been involved in civil rights cases. We are filing welfare cases involving the man-in-the-house rule and the employable mother rule; housing cases, involving the right of public housing officials to evict without a hearing or to refuse to house mothers with illegitimate children. There is litigation over the right of poor persons in private housing to defend eviction proceedings without having to post a bond in twice the amount of the rent. In criminal prosecutions, there is the issue of whether an indigent may be released without bail where an affluent person would have been released because he had the money to put up bail. Cases are asserting the right of an accused misdemeanant to request and have granted court appointed counsel, and so forth.

But for lawyers, the history of civil rights teaches us something about technique as well as substance. The school segregation cases and other leading civil rights litigation were successful for a variety of reasons, not the least of which was that the law had to develop along with the moral and social needs of the times. We know also, however, that courts do not merely register moral judgments; they pass upon the substance and technique of a litigation. A case with a good record brought according to the proper procedure, at the right time, will bring better results than something quickly tossed together and rushed into court. But that bad case often can, and often does, make a precedent which will undercut the good case that otherwise might have carried the day.

Many romantic tales have been told about how the civil rights cases of the past generation were conducted — as if by computer from some stainless steel combat information center. In fact, there were plans which on numerous occasions were changed. There were spur of the moment decisions which deviated from preconceived notions. The original plan in 1933 was to bring a large number of separate-but-equal cases at the elementary and high school level, and, by economic pressure, force the South into integration. As the plan was finally formulated, it was changed to a constitutional attack on segregation under the theory of *Yick Wo v. Hopkins*, that is, that the segregation laws, in fact, were implemented unequally universally and therefore were unconstitutional.

As the campaign got rolling, it ignored elementary and high schools and concentrated on law schools, and indeed upon states with white law schools and no Negro ones. Yet before the decisions in *Sweatt* and *McLaurin*, which outlawed segregation in graduate and professional schools, the elementary and high school cases were already underway. But those cases proceeded alternatively on two theories: (1) physical inequality and (2) the charge that segregation *per se* was unconstitutional. Following *Sweatt* and *McLaurin* we took a cue from some of the considerations that went into those decisions, and social science testimony was introduced as well.

But the one thing that the cases had in common was that they were *considered*. They were considered with regard to one another, to their sequence, and to their theories. Sometimes they were brought consistently with one another and sometimes deliberately inconsistently, offering options to the courts.

As we now move into an era of poverty law, which today is in some senses comparable to the civil rights law of the mid-thirties, we ought to reflect on that experience. There are differences and similarities. Obviously, many of the questions that individuals, government funded offices, privately financed offices serving the poor, and others face is that many of the legal questions we deal with are not susceptible to treatment that is consistent nationally. Many questions are questions of state law, such as the validity of an installment sales contract at unconscionable rates of interest. However, even as to issues like these, state courts often follow one another.

Some state courts are held in higher regard than others. Some are more readily persuasible to our views than others. Where uniform legislation is involved, there is a strong tendency toward uniformity of judicial treatment. Some stem from national law, such as those arising from state enforcement of federal welfare regulations. Some are of constitutional dimension, such as the question of whether a public housing authority may evict a tenant without notice and hearing contrary to the due process clause of the Fourteenth Amendment.

It would be illusory to think that the many different individuals and groups handling poverty law litigation could possibly coordinate the thousands of cases that we will be handling each year. But certainly we ought to be thinking about the same issues. We all ought to be aware that the consequences of an isolated litigation may radiate beyond a particular community. We ought to take benefit from the experience of our brothers in similar cases. We ought to be exposed to the best thinking that exists on the issues we worry about. We ought to communicate with one another to see what effect one case, or one approach, or one theory may have on another — and perhaps on the country as a whole.

Central to what we do in so uncharted an area are the questions of what difference our lawsuits will make in law and society — questions of social priority and social effectiveness. Jerome Carlin and his associates have dared to pose the problems we must probe and how and when we should delve into them. Rarely, if ever, have such provoking questions been put at the outset of a legal undertaking. If we pursue only some of them, we shall have laid a sound foundation for a legal structure that will shape the quality of American life for generations to come.

JACK GREENBERG
*Director-Counsel N.A.A.C.P. Legal Defense and
Educational Fund.*

June, 1967
New York, N. Y.

PREFACE

In 1963 The Center for the Study of Law and Society accepted a grant from the Russell Sage Foundation for the purpose of examining issues and perspectives bearing on the administration of civil justice. It was hoped that some ground might be laid for research that would be of interest to social scientists and of value for legal reform.

The civil justice project stimulated considerable exploratory research and dialogue at Berkeley, involving lawyers, political scientists, and sociologists, especially regarding the nature of the adversary principle and its place within a developing legal order; the wide variety of settings, private as well as public, within which justice is administered; the significance of the administrative process for the quality of justice and for legal change; the ethics of the legal profession; the emergent structure of court systems and the capacity of courts as we know them to deal with new problems, such as mass trials of civil rights demonstrators; the interplay of criminal and civil justice, as in welfare administration. A continuing theme and question was the ability of our legal institutions to change and to serve as effective vehicles of social change in other segments of society.

As discussion proceeded, it became evident that the field of law and poverty should be of central concern to social scientists and lawyers, not only for its practical significance but because so many of the more general problems affecting the quality of justice are highlighted in that context. Therefore it was decided to undertake a comprehensive review of what is known about the administration of justice to the poor, with a view to identifying issues for debate and discussion, issues that would stimulate questioning and policy-relevant research.

Civil Justice for the Poor, reprinted here from the November 1966 issue of the *Law and Society Review*, is a report of that inquiry. It suggests that the administration of justice cannot be separated from the quality of the substantive law affecting the poor; that mass-production justice, the paternalism of welfare programs, and the political weakness of the poor tend to weaken or attenuate standards of procedural justice; and that legal representation has been, in this field, inadequate to the task. A major emphasis is the need to increase the civic competence of the poor as a condition of their effective participation in the legal order.

In our time, there is an increasing demand for justice of high quality. This demand, being made by ever-larger numbers and by groups that have hitherto been largely silent and unheard, will test and try our legal institutions. It is fitting that we do all we can to enlarge the commitment and awareness of those who might be able to help meet, in their own way, the foreseeable crises of social understanding and of social policy. We are grateful to the Russell Sage Foundation for its support of that effort.

JEROME E. CARLIN, JAN HOWARD,
and SHELDON L. MESSINGER

June, 1967
Berkeley, California

CIVIL JUSTICE AND THE POOR
Issues for Sociological Research

Jerome E. Carlin
Jan Howard
Sheldon L. Messinger

In this report on civil justice and the poor we seek to examine issues relevant to the sociology of law. We have studied law and poverty because this area seems to us most likely to call into question conventional assumptions about the structure, conditions and consequences of legal administration. Here, we believe, the actual operation of the legal system is most likely to deviate from received notions; and at this stage of inquiry gross deviations may be most useful in stimulating research issues and perspectives. We have emphasized the civil instead of the criminal side because sociologists have given it so little attention.

This report is based on a survey of recent social science and legal literature supplemented by exploratory observations of the dealings of various agencies with the poor, and by selected interviews with attorneys and other legal functionaries. Examination of these materials confirms the widespread impression that

AUTHORS' NOTE: This monograph is part of a continuing effort at the Center for the Study of Law and Society, University of California, Berkeley, to formulate a program of research on the administration of civil justice. The project has been supported by a grant from the Russell Sage Foundation. An earlier report stemming from this project is: Jerome E. Carlin and Jan Howard, *Legal Representation and Class Justice,*[12] U.C.L.A. Law Review, 381-437 (1965). We wish to acknowledge the valuable contribution of the following research assistants whose observations and interviews are partly incorporated in the body of the report: Jan Hermes, Ian Kennedy, Frederic LeClercq, Aryay Lenske and Nancy Lichtenstein. Ann Fagan Ginger and Harvey Wittenberg helped· document the section on the law. We also wish to thank our colleagues Philip Selzick, Harold Wilensky and Philippe Nonet for their many substantive as well as editorial suggestions.

the poor are less likely than the rich to enjoy the benefits and protections accorded by the law. Four aspects of the problem are considered: (1) the character of the law as it concerns the poor; (2) the treatment of the poor by courts and other legal agencies; (3) the legal representation received by the poor; and (4) the capacity of the poor to use the legal system.

The poor, as we have said, generally obtain less protection from the law than the rich. It seems clear from the literature that they have no less need for such protection. Even a brief catalogue suggests that they have many grievances that are proper matters for legal consideration.

To begin with, the poor are frequently in market situations where illegal practices prevail.[1] Consumer fraud, for example, is widely prevalant and takes many forms, including misrepresentation of price, of quality, and even of the identity of the seller. The low-income consumer is particularly susceptible to these abuses.[2] The cost of credit is very commonly disguised and the poor are apparently most often deceived.[3] Furthermore, the collection practices used against the poor are harsh, often illegal, and sometimes amount to sheer extortion.[4]

---

1. We recognize, of course, that the poor themselves are often moved by their economic and social situation to engage in illegal practices.

2. See D. CAPLOVITZ, THE POOR PAY MORE 142-45 (1963). Also note the following:

> In this "captive" [consumer] market, unethical practices flourish: "bait advertising," "switch sales," reconditioned goods sold as new, tie-in "contest" prizes. Exchanges are virtually unknown; the buyer is "stuck" with his bad bargain.

P. WALD, LAW AND POVERTY 1965 24 (1965). For a description of various techniques used to disguise price in the automobile market, see *Why Auto Dealers Don't Like Cash Buyers*, 30 CONSUMER REPORTS 258-61 (1965). Although the poor are not the only ones subject to such abuses, they appear to be most vulnerable to the deceptions involved.

3. CONSUMER REPORTS notes that "In the present market, the rate of credit charges is usually concealed and, even when it is revealed, comparisons are difficult because the rates are stated in too many different ways." See *Interest Rates*, 29 CONSUMER REPORTS 504-05 (1964). A recent study of a sophisticated group of middle class consumers (subscribers to CONSUMER REPORTS) showed that few (18%) knew either the true annual rate of interest they were paying or the percentage of principal they paid as interest. Those who knew the true rate of interest paid least for credit; the totally ignorant group paid most. See *Id.* at 505. It seems reasonable to assume that poor subjects would have tended to fall in the latter group, among those totally ignorant of the cost of credit.

4. Patricia Wald notes:

> The collections necessary to stay in business are achieved by a variety of coercive devices. Garnishment threats are effective. What is at stake often is the purchaser's job. Employers, particularly in low-skilled, high-turnover employment, are loathe to bother with wage attachments; firing is easier. Creditors

The law of contract is a weak reed for the poor man. Slum landlords are notoriously delinquent in fulfilling their obligations to provide services and repairs. These owners, it has been noted:

> feel little economic pressure to keep their low-income housing repaired and habitable, or to rehabilitate badly deteriorated buildings. Poor tenants complain of housing code violations and are evicted, but they cannot move away. They are immobilized by lack of funds or by their race.[5]

Merchants often fail to provide bargained-for merchandise or refuse to honor their warranties.[6] Insurance settlements and cancellations involving poor persons are apparently rarely challenged through legal channels, but reportedly they are often questionable if not frankly illegal.[7]

The poor also suffer because agencies of government fail to fulfill their legal responsibilities. Inadequate housing code enforcement is a well-known example.[8] Other commonly recognized abuses in slum neighborhoods include poorly kept streets, infrequently collected garbage, dilapidated and insufficiently manned schools, lack of police protection and over zealous "law enforcement."[9] Moreover, government efforts to help the poor bring in their train a host of dubious practices. Some urban renewal projects deal high-handedly with those who are displaced;[10]

> threaten to report purchasers to the welfare authorities; relief recipients are not supposed to buy on credit. The original sales contract is often sold to a finance company or collection agent against whom the buyer can raise no equitable defenses.

See P. Wald, *op. cit. supra* note 2. See also Note, *Project: Legislative Regulation of Retail Installment Financing*, 7 U.C.L.A. L. REV. 741-42 (1960); D. Caplovitz, *op. cit. supra* note 2, 189-90, for discussion of illegal collection practices on the part of law enforcement officials themselves.

5. P. Wald, *op. cit. supra* note 2, at 14.

6. Caplovitz observes that "when the low-income consumer fails to live up to his obligations of payment, the merchant is able to utilize the law to protect his rights. When the merchant fails to respect a guarantee, however, the consumer is more likely to lose his initial investment than to obtain justice." D. Caplovitz, *op. cit. supra* note 2, at 151.

7. L. Fuller, *American Legal Realism*, 82 U. PA. L. REV. 438-42 (1934).

8. See Note, *Enforcement of Municipal Housing Codes*, 79 HARV. L. REV. 801 (1965); J. Levi, "The Legal Needs of the Poor: Problems Relating to Real Property," paper read at the National Conference on Law and Poverty, Washington, D.C., June 23-25, 1965.

9. See THE GOVERNOR'S COMMISSION ON THE LOS ANGELES RIOTS, VIOLENCE IN THE CITY — AN END OR A BEGINNING (1965).

10. See, *e.g.,* P. Hauser & M. Wirth, *Relocation — Opportunity or Liability?* in POVERTY IN AMERICA 360 (M. Gordon ed. 1965); Note, *Protecting the Standing of Renewal Site Families to Seek Review of Community Relocation Planning*, 73 YALE L.J. 1080 (1964); E. Richey, *Tenant Oppression: Our Smoldering Housing Scandal*, 24 THE ANTIOCH REV. 337 (1964); H. GANS, THE URBAN VILLAGERS 281-335 (1962).

public housing administrators invoke restrictive and perhaps illegal requirements for tenancy, and their eviction of poor families is often arbitrary.[11] Denial, reduction and termination of welfare benefits on vague, unarticulated or clearly illegal grounds is apparently widespread;[12] methods used to check continuing eligibility have also been attacked as legally questionable if not unconstitutional.[13]

What are the conditions that help to explain the pervasive and persistent character of these practices? We turn first to an examination of the law.

THE CHARACTER OF LAW AFFECTING THE POOR

It has long been argued that the law[14] is not a neutral instrument, but rather that it is oriented in favor of those groups or classes in society having the power to bend the legal order to their advantage.[15] The contention is that today as in the past the law primarily serves to protect and enhance the rights and interests of property holders and those in positions of wealth and authority. Three types of bias are considered: (1) favored parties; (2) dual law — *de jure* denial of equal protection; (3) *de facto* denial of equal protection.

FAVORED PARTIES

The law frequently favors certain parties or roles in a relationship, and the poor are less likely than the rich to be found in these roles. Thus, substantive and procedural law benefits and protects landlords over tenants, and lenders over bor-

---

11. See E. Sparer, *The New Public Law: The Relation of Indigents to State Administration* in THE EXTENSION OF LEGAL SERVICES TO THE POOR 23-40 (U.S. Dept. of HEW 1964).

12. An indication of the range of questionable grounds may be seen in P. Wald, *op. cit. supra* note 2, at 30-32.

13. See C. Reich, *Midnight Welfare Searches and the Social Security Act*, 72 YALE L.J. 1346 (1963); C. Reich, *The New Property*, 73 YALE L.J. 733 (1964); C. Reich, *Individual Rights and Social Welfare: The Emerging Legal Issues*, 74 YALE L.J. 1245 (1965); E. Sparer, *The Role of the Welfare Client's Lawyer*, 12 U.C.L.A. L. REV. 361 (1965); Brief for Appellants, Parrish v. Civil Service Comm'n.

14. As the term *law* is used here, it refers to the common law, statutes, rules, and decisions laid down by legislative, administrative and judicial bodies, and informal agreements that are binding on decision-makers. We recognize that law is often made in the process of its administration. Consequently there can be no hard and fast line between studies of the law itself and studies of its administration.

15. F. ENGELS, THE ORIGIN OF THE FAMILY, PRIVATE PROPERTY AND THE STATE (1942); K. RENNER, THE INSTITUTIONS OF PRIVATE LAW AND THEIR SOCIAL FUNCTIONS (O. Kahn-Freund ed. 1949).

rowers.[16, 17] Let us examine these two examples of favored party bias in the law.

Landlord-Tenant. The common law has generally promoted the interests of the landlord against the tenant; this has had a special impact on poor tenants living in slums. According to traditional legal doctrine the tenant's obligation to pay rent is independent of his lessor's covenants to repair and maintain the premises.[18] Thus, unless there are statutes to the contrary, the tenant cannot withhold rent as a means of compelling landlord compliance with health and safety codes or contractual obligations.[19] This posture of the common law has particular rele-

16. We recognize that poor persons do occasionally assume the roles of landlord and lender; they may, for example, lend money to friends or rent out rooms as a means of supplementing their income.

17. The particular problems of poor tenants and borrowers are the result of a combination of favored party and *de facto* bias. Their disadvantaged position rests in part on the favored party bias of the law; it is accentuated by their generally insecure and vulnerable situation. As borrowers, for example, the poor are more likely to have a large proportion of their income tied up in debt payments than the wealthy, and they are less likely to have any savings. (G. KATONA, SURVEY OF CONSUMER FINANCES 43, 53-54 [1962]; D. Caplovitz, *op. cit. supra* note 2, at 111.) The fact that they are such bad risks means that the poor are especially vulnerable to exploitative credit practices. Consequently, they are most likely to be disadvantaged by ineffective usury laws.

18. See J. Levi, *supra* note 8, at 1; N. LeBlanc, "Why Tenants Need Lawyers," paper presented at the Conference on the Extension of Legal Services to the Poor, Washington, D.C., Nov. 12, 1964, 11-12; E. Richey, *supra* note 10, at 341-42; Note, *supra* note 8, at 844, 845, where it is observed that "most suggested changes in landlord-tenant law are variations of one basic theme, suspension of the duty of the tenant to pay the rent when uncorrected housing code violations exist"; J. Fossum, *Rent Withholding*, 53 CALIF. L. REV. 304, 313 (1965). See also Fossum's general discussion of "the inadequacy to the slum tenant of personal rights of action." *Id.* at 310-14. He notes that "the common law armed the tenant with little that would insure him that his dwelling would be kept in a comfortable or even habitable condition." *Id.* at 310.

It is, of course, also true that in the absence of a covenant to repair, the landlord owes his tenant no duty of maintenance. According to Fossum this rule has become so firmly entrenched in the law that it is improbable that it will be altered without legislative intervention. He suggests that viewing the situation realistically, the burden for making major repairs and improvements ought to be upon the lessor because he is in the better financial position and has the greater financial interest in maintaining the quality of the dwelling. *Id.* at 311.

19. In some jurisdictions there are statutes which permit rent to be withheld as a means of forcing the landlord to make repairs and provide essential services. But these statutes are generally inadequate. In New York, for example, Section 755 of the Real Property Actions and Proceedings Law permits the tenant to pay his rent to the court until violations of the code are corrected. However, it has been argued that "although Section 755 is a powerful defense, . . . it does not actually provide substantial relief to the tenants since during the time that the violations continue the tenants are still required to pay the full rent, even though they are not receiving a full consideration or return for their rent." N.

vance to the poor because they often live in vermin-infested substandard housing where landlords perpetually fail to provide needed services and repairs.[20]

To correct some of the injustices resulting from strict application of the common law the courts have developed the fiction of a constructive eviction by the landlord when his breach of contractual obligations denies the tenant beneficial use and enjoyment of the premises. Thus, under certain circumstances the tenant may be permitted to abandon the premises without further liability.[21] However, as Fossum puts it: "The right to move out is an empty one for the people in the slums."[22] This fact has prompted some to argue that the court should recognize a tenant

---

LeBlanc, *supra* note 18, at 9-11. See J. Levy, *supra* note 8, at 9; J. Fossum, *supra* note 18, at 324-27; Note, *supra* note 8, at 845-46. Whether the 1965 amendment to the Section will appreciably increase its effectiveness remains to be seen. For a statement of the new law, see N.Y. REAL PROPERTY ACTIONS AND PROCEEDINGS § 755. A few states have enacted "repair and deduct" laws which generally provide that if the landlord fails to make certain repairs upon demand the tenant may make them himself and deduct the cost from the rent or vacate without further liability. See J. Fossum, *supra* note 18, at 312. In two states (California and Montana) the charge against the landlord cannot exceed one month's rent, which is often not enough to cover the cost of repairs. Furthermore, the landlord can contract away the obligations imposed by such statutes, and, thus, he can shift his duty of repair onto the tenant. *Ibid.*

It should also be noted that departments of welfare have withheld rent as a weapon against slum landlords. This type of rent withholding began in Chicago in 1961 and spread to New York State where it was introduced via state law in 1962. See *Withholding Rent: New Weapon Added to Arsenal for War on Slumlords*, 21 J. OF HOUSING 67-72 (1964); Note, *supra* note 8, at 842-43; J. Fosum, *supra* note 18, at 327-31.

20. In 1961 Cook County, Ill., welfare officials estimated that of the approximately 5.2 million dollars paid out each month for relief rental allowances, one million went for substandard housing. J. OF HOUSING, *supra* note 19, at 67. And in 1964 in New York City Welfare Commissioner Dumpson estimated that of the 78 million dollars paid out annually for welfare rents, 33 million was paid for substandard housing. *Id.* at 69. See also Richey, *op. cit, supra* note 10.

21. J. Fossum, *supra* note 18, at 313. The doctrine of *implied warranty* has also been used to protect the tenant. In Pines v. Perssion, 14 Wis. 2d 509, 111 N.W. 2d 409 (1961), the tenant was allowed to vacate the premises and recover the rent deposited less a reasonable amount for the period of actual occupance. The landmark case here is Ingalls v. Hobbs, 156 Mass. 348, 31 N.E. 286 (1892), where the court held, with respect to the lease of a completely furnished house for a single season, that there is an implied warranty that the house is fit for immediate habitation.

Although the doctrine of implied warranty has generally been applied only to short-term leases of furnished premises, it has been extended to include unfurnished apartments in multiple units. See Recent Decisions, *Landlord and Tenant — Application of Implied Warranty*, 45 MARQ. L. REV. 630-33 (1962); P. Blawie, *Implied Warranty of Fitness for Habitation of Furnished Premises for a Short Period of Time*, 33 CONN. B. J. 55-61 (1959).

22. J. Fossum, *supra* note 18, at 314. See Note, *supra* note 8, at 844.

defense of failure of consideration when landlords violate their obligations. Then the tenant could either rescind the contract and abandon the premises or pay a pro rata reduction in rent.[23] Giving tenants this option would be a step toward equalizing protections of the law.

It has been observed that tax law benefits the slum landlord to the detriment of the tenant. Julian Levi contends that, "If the tenement is old and in bad condition, allowable depreciation under the Internal Revenue Code will be high; while poor condition and deterioration will be recognized by the real estate tax assessor as the occasion for reducing appraised values."[24]

Procedural law as well as substantive law may be biased in favor of the landlord. For example, New York requires a violation of record before tenants can invoke certain defenses against landlords who have failed to provide essential services.[25] This requirement may subvert the rights of tenants because of the difficulties involved in establishing an official record of violation.[26] Thus, it is argued that the

---

23. See N. LeBlanc, *supra* note 18, at 11-12; Brief for Tenant-Appellant, Kuperberg v. Cruz, New York Supreme Court, Appellate Term — First Department (Mimeographed). Two major points are made in this brief: (1) "Where grounds for constructive eviction exist but where because of an extreme housing shortage the tenant is unable to abandon the premises, traditional common law rules of constructive eviction without abandonment should be modified to permit the remedy of constructive eviction" and (2) "The failure of a landlord of a multiple dwelling to provide essential services and facilities to a tenant as required by law constitutes a partial failure of consideration which should entitle a tenant to pay only a pro rata part of the rent."

Kuperberg v. Cruz was decided against the tenant-defendant Cruz at the trial level. On appeal to the Appellate Term it was again decided against Cruz, with no opinion being rendered by the Court. The lawyers for Cruz then requested leave to appeal to the Appellate Division. This request was denied by the Appellate Term without opinion.

In April, 1965, when we were last in correspondence with Nancy LeBlanc, who argued the case before the Appellate Term, she commented "except for the advancement of the argument, we have made no change in the law of landlord-tenant re 'failure of consideration.'" Personal communication from Nancy E. LeBlanc, Associate Director, Legal Services Unit, Mobilization for Youth, Inc., April 12, 1965.

24. J. Levi, *supra* note 8, at 3, 5. On the matter of income tax law and slums, see A. Sporn, *Some Contributions of the Income Tax Law to the Growth and Prevalence of Slums*, 59 COLUM. L. REV. 1026 (1959), in which he considers those aspects of our income tax policy which seem to him to have a propensity to generate and maintain slums. See also the critique of Sporn in W. Blum & A. Dunham, *Income Tax Law and Slums: Some Further Reflections*, 60 COLUM. L. REV. 447-53 (1960); and Sporn's rejoinder, A. Sporn, *Slums and the Income Tax — A Brief Rejoinder*, 60 COLUM. L. REV. 454-57 (1960).

25. See N. LeBlanc, *supra* note 18, at 10-11.

26. On the lax enforcement of housing codes in slum areas, see E. Richey, *supra* note 10, at 340, 341, 345. Tenants who report code violations to public officials may be evicted.

court should look to the actual condition of the dwelling, not simply to violations of record.[27]

Public housing laws are also said to be biased against the tenant. According to Cloward and Elman:

> Legislation is written in such a way as to deny tenants any of the rights commonly associated with tenancy in private housing. Apartments can be inspected at will by management; leases are month to month; eviction can occur without recourse to the courts.[28]

Sparer contends that in some places the housing authority reserves the right to evict without giving any reason whatsoever.[29]

Borrower-Lender. In the consumer area favored-party bias is perhaps most clearly seen in the creditor-debtor relationship. With respect to laws governing interest rates it has been observed that "such interest ceilings as legislatures impose on retail installment credit and small loans . . . are set at the behest of credit extenders and without study."[30] Further, the contention is that "few states have any real penalties for usury,"[31] that generally the sanctions are too mild to discourage illegal lenders.[32] Usury laws may also be rendered ineffective by exemp-

---

In Chicago those who had suffered such reprisal appealed to the Illinois legislature which then passed a law making such eviction illegal, *Id.* at 349-50.

27. See N. LeBlanc, *supra* note 18, at 10-11.

28. R. Cloward & R. Elman, *Poverty, Injustice and the Welfare State: How Rights can Be Secured*, 202 THE NATION 264 (March 7, 1966).

29. E. Sparer, *supra* note 11, at 35-36. See also Sparer's discussion of bias in housing authority rules of procedure. *Id.* at 36-37, and C. Reich, *Individual Rights, supra* note 13, at 1250.

The practice of drawing leases on a month to month basis is recommended by the Federal Housing and Home Agency to permit "any necessary evictions to be accomplished with a minimum of delay and expense on the giving of a statutory notice to quit without stating the reason for such notice." See E. Sparer, *supra* note 11, at 35-36. Sparer questions the legality of a housing manager's quiet refusal to state reasons for terminating a tenancy, because where housing authorities choose to *assert* an arbitrary reason, it has been held that they have exceeded their legal power. *Id.* at 36.

30. G. Brunn, "Legal Aspects of the Rights of Creditors and Debtors," p. 8 (paper presented at a Seminar on Research Needs in Consumer Economics, Sept. 11, 1964, Univ. of Calif., Berkeley).

31. See C. Neal, The Known and Unknown in Consumer Credit, p. 8 (paper presented at a Seminar on Research Needs in Consumer Economics, Sept. 11, 1964, Univ. of Calif., Berkeley).

32. See W. Mors, *Small Loan Laws* 1-2 Cleveland, Bureau of Business Research, Western Reserve Univ., 1961, Educational Pamphlet No. 2, where it is observed that usury laws neither prohibit lending nor protect consumers.

tion provisions. According to Brunn such provisions in the California constitution exempt almost everyone professionally in the business of lending money.[33] Moreover creditors can obtain special state permits or licenses which allow them to charge more than the basic usury rate. Neal argues that most lenders today have such permits. "Banks, credit unions, loan companies, finance companies, and even retailers, now can charge more than the simple interest rate defined as 'tops' under state usury codes."[34]

There are many other loopholes favoring the creditor. For example, credit extended by a seller is not generally subject to the provisions of interest and usury statutes, the theory being that the vendor is not engaged in lending money but in selling goods. The credit charge is supposedly not interest. It merely represents the difference between the cash price and the installment price.[35]

Laws concerning remedies for missed payments may also favor the creditor. In some jurisdictions, he is allowed two remedies — repossession and deficiency judgment. Some observers believe this gives an unfair advantage to the creditor.[36]

DUAL LAW — DE JURE DENIAL OF EQUAL PROTECTION

A second kind of bias is seen in the development of separate and unequal systems of law for the poor and for certain racial minorities. As a result, many lower class whites and Negroes are in effect relegated to a position of second-class citizen-

---

33. See Brunn, *supra* note 30, at 2. The California Constitution sets maximum interest rates at 10 per cent, but various financial and lending institutions such as building and loan associations, credit unions, pawn brokers and personal property brokers are exempt. The legislature is given the power to control and fix the rate of interest these exempt groups may charge. CALIF. CONST, art. 20, § 22.

34. See C. Neal, *supra* note 31, at 9.

35. See B. CURRAN (American Bar Foundation), TRENDS IN CONSUMER CREDIT LEGIS-LATION 13 (1965). The court does not always accept this interpretation. For example, in a series of cases from 1952 to 1957, the Arkansas Supreme Court decided that finance charges made in connection with sale of goods could be attacked for usury if the return exceeded maximum contract charges permitted for loan of money. Thus in this jurisdiction finance charges for the extension of credit by a seller are considered interest, and the customary distinction between lender and vendor credit disappears by judicial fiat. *Id.* at 2, ch IV.

36. Under the California Retail Installment Sales Act which covers all retail installment sales except automobiles, the creditor is no longer allowed the two remedies. CAL. CIVIL CODE § 1801 *et. seq.* He must elect either to sue for the balance due without repossessing the goods or to repossess the goods. He cannot do both. However, under the Automobile Sales Act which covers sales of automobiles, the creditor can still invoke the double remedy.

ship. Such persons are denied *de jure* the protections and benefits which the law provides for middle and upper class whites.[37] To the extent that *de jure* discrimination arises from or is supported by "state action," it may of course be challenged under the Fourteenth Amendment.

According to tenBroek there are two separate systems of family law, one for the poor and one for those in comfortable circumstances.[38] The rules differ with respect to property and support relations of husband and wife, creation and termination of the marital relationship and responsibility for the support of relatives.[39] His contention is that the family law of the rich is "civil family law," created, developed and administered by the courts — not designed in either substantive provision or judicial administration to meet the needs of the poor.[40] The family law of the poor is public law, administered largely through state and local non-judicial agencies, and more concerned with minimizing the costs of relief than maximizing the rights and interests of recipients.[41] TenBroek asks whether a dual system of family law is less unequal than school racial segregation, generating among recipients a feeling of inferiority that may affect the hearts and minds of the poor in ways unlikely ever to be undone.[42]

---

37. One way of viewing this particular form of bias is to argue that certain roles like welfare recipient are only played by the poor and that discriminatory laws are applied to them. Another approach, and the one we follow here, is to argue that certain roles are similar or the same for rich and poor, *e.g.*, spouse, father, recipient of government funds, school child, but that different laws are applied to them in these roles.

This approach then, differs from that adopted in our discussion of favored party bias where we stress the different roles played by rich and poor, and *de facto* bias where we emphasize the different capacities of rich and poor to realize benefits the law presumably provides for all classes. Here we contend that the law is biased to the extent that different laws are applied to those who are presumed to be equals; to the extent it can be shown that they should not be treated as equals, the dual law criticism loses its force. See, in this regard, T. Lewis & R. Levy, "Family Law and Welfare Policies — The Case for 'Dual System'" (paper presented for the Conference on the Law of the Poor, U. of Calif., Berkeley, Feb. 17-19, 1966).

38. See J. tenBroek, *California's Dual System of Family Law: Its Origin, Development, and Present Status*, 16 Stan. L. Rev. pt. 1 at 257-58 (1964).

39. J. tenBroek, *California's Dual System of Family Law: Its Origin, Development, and Present Status*, 17 Stan. L. Rev. pt. 3 at 614 (1965).

40. J. tenBroek, *supra* note 38, at 257-313; J. tenBroek, *California's Dual System of Family Law: Its Origin, Development, and Present Status*, 16 Stan. L. Rev. pt. 2 at 900-81 (1964).

41. *Ibid.*

42. J. tenBroek, *supra* note 38, pt. 1 at 258.

The dual law argument applies to welfare law in general. In considering many types of welfare programs (*e.g.*, public assistance, unemployment insurance, public housing), Reich contends that the government has one set of rules for dispensing benefits to the poor and another for dispensing largess to the rich (*e.g.*, licenses, subsidies, contracts). He argues that entitlement to government largess is less likely to be protected as a right when the recipient is poor,[43] and concludes that this constitutes a denial of equal protection under the federal constitution.

The classic cases of dual law affecting the poor are laws which discriminate against Negroes and other racial or national minorities. Such laws have a special impact on the poor, because many of them are non-white.[44] As a result of government action, *de jure* discrimination against Negroes has been appreciably reduced, but it is still a widespread phenomenon. Segregation of public schools will continue

---

43. C. Reich, *Individual Rights, supra* note 13, at 1245. See also Reich, *The New Property, op. cit., supra* note 13, at 785, where he says that "the concept of right is most urgently needed with respect to benefits like unemployment compensation, public assistance, and old age insurance."

Elizabeth Wickenden argues that the very heart of the poverty problem in the United States in one of *entitlement* under law. "In the relationship of individuals to the society in which they live, dignity, freedom, and security rest upon a maximum range of objectively defined rights and entitlements," E. Wickenden, *The Indigent and Welfare Administration,* THE EXTENSION OF LEGAL SERVICES TO THE POOR 41, 46 (U.S. Dept. of HEW, 1964). See E. Wickenden, *Administration of Welfare Rights,* pp. 5-9, paper prepared for National Conference on Law and Poverty, Washington, D.C., June 24, 1965.

Welfare law tends to place broad, unrestrained power in the hands of administrators because certain provisions of the law are vague, and because administrative regulations are often overly detailed and therefore difficult it not impossible to apply. One reason for the vagueness of welfare law is that it is rarely put to the test of judicial or administrative review; as a result "rights that might have been developed out of existing welfare statutes have atrophied from disuse." (Reich, *Individual Rights and Social Welfare, supra,* p. 1256).

44. Of the total number of families in the United States in 1963, approximately 10 per cent were non-white; of families in poverty (those with incomes under $3,000) about 25 per cent were non-white. Further, 43 per cent of non-white families were defined as poor in 1963, compared to 16 per cent of white families. See H. Miller, *Changes in the Number and Composition of the Poor,* in POVERTY IN AMERICA 86-87 (M. Gordon ed. 1965). See also K. Davis, *Some Demographic Aspects of Poverty in the United States,* in *id.* at 310.

A very high proportion of welfare recipients are non-white. In New York City, for example, Welfare Commissioner Dumpson estimates that Negroes and Puerto Ricans constitute 75 per cent of the recipients. See *City Fights Holding Action on Poverty,* N.Y. *Times,* Nov. 15, 1964, p. 84.

to be legal in many localities of the South for some time to come.[45, 46] And the court has ruled that tax exempt private schools can discriminate if the founder of the charitable trust specified discrimination as a condition of the trust.[47] In certain sections of the South the semi-official Parent-Teachers Associations exclude from membership all parents and teachers from segregated Negro schools and they do so legally.[48] Private hospitals can discriminate or segregate unless public subsidies are involved.[49] And discrimination in employment is illegal only in industries cov-

45. It should be noted that Brown v. Board of Education, 347 U.S. 483 (1954); 349 U.S. 294 (1955), which authorized integration of public schools "with all deliberate speed" has had little overall impact on segregation in the deep South. At the present time only 1 out of 13 Negro pupils in that region attends school with whites. See San Francisco CHRONICLE, February 16, 1966, p. 8.

46. Title VI of the Civil Rights Act of 1964 specifies that no person shall be subjected to racial discrimination under any program or activity receiving federal financial assistance; and the Department of Health, Education, and Welfare has begun to implement this act with respect to federal aid to education. Whether the Civil Rights Act provision will appreciably expedite integration of public schools in the South remains to be seen.

47. The landmark case here is In Re Girard College Trusteeship, 391 Pa. 434 (1958), cert. denied 357 U.S. 570 (1958). The Board of Trustees which operated Girard College was an agency of the State of Pennsylvania. For it to enforce the whites-only discriminatory clause of the Girard trust was ruled a violation of the 14th Amendment. So the public trustees were replaced by private (non-State) trustees, and they then enforced the discriminatory provision of the will. The general rule of trust law which was applied was that if the trust is affected by the character or disability of the trustee, then he will be replaced and the trust saved. A trust will not fail because of the disability of the trustee.

More recently the Supreme Court of the United States barred the City of Macon, Georgia, from withdrawing as trustees of a park to allow the park to operate as a "private" facility and to discriminate against Negroes. Whether this posture of the court will eventually affect discrimination in private schools remains to be seen. See N.Y. TIMES, Jan. 18, 1966, p. 1.

Parenthetically, it should be noted that there is legal precedent for private schools to ignore the discriminatory clauses in their trusts. In Rice University v. Carr (1964), an action was brought by Rice University in a Texas court against the Attorney General of the state, seeking a judgment authorizing the University to depart from restrictions in the original trust and charter which prohibited it from admitting Negro students. A jury made special findings of fact to the effect that the wishes of the founder to create a first-class educational institution could not be realized if racial restrictions were adhered to and enforced. Final judgment was entered authorizing the University to admit qualified students without regard to color or race. 9 RACE REL. L. REP. 613, Spring 1964.

48. We are using the concept "legal discrimination" to mean discrimination which has not been declared illegal, even if cases are pending.

49. For a ruling to the effect that hospitals cannot discriminate if they are receiving federal funds, see Simkins v. Moses H. Cone Memorial Hosp. 323 F.2d 1959 (4th Cir. 1963).

ered by fair employment laws.[50] Furthermore, discrimination is permitted in almost all private housing sold or rented in the United States[51] although prohibited in public housing as a form of state action.[52] The situation is less clear in housing partly financed through state aid.[53]

DE FACTO BIAS

A third type of bias in the law may be termed *de facto* bias. On paper the law treats rich and poor alike, but in fact the correlates of poverty make equality impossible. Ehrlich suggests that *de jure* equality may actually accentuate *de facto* inequality. He argues that "the more the rich and the poor are dealt with according to the same legal propositions, the more the advantage of the rich is increased."[54]

De facto bias is pervasive because so many correlates of poverty such as indigency, ignorance or insecurity can serve as barriers to justice. In essence it is bias by default. It represents a failure of the law to take into account the differential

---

50. The federal government has for some time prohibited discrimination in federal employment and in employment on federal contracts. The 1964 Civil Rights Act, 78 Stat. 253, 42 U.S.C. § 2000e(b) (1964), prohibits discrimination in industries affecting commerce providing they have 25 or more employees. Actually, the first year after the effective date of the act industries having fewer than 100 employees are exempt; the second year those with fewer than 75 are exempt; but eventually the figure "25" will be relevant.

51. California's attempt to limit discrimination in private housing was overruled by public referendum in 1964. The legality of the referendum measure (Proposition 14, an amendment to the California Constitution) is being reviewed by the courts.

52. See D. King, *Housing: The Right to Occupancy Without Discrimination* in LEGAL ASPECTS OF THE CIVIL RIGHTS MOVEMENT 133 (D. King & C. Quick eds. 1965).

53. According to King, "The Supreme Court has yet to pass upon the effect of many of these aspects of less direct [governmental] participation in, or assistance to, housing and their relation to discrimination." *Id.* at 134. However, in 1950 the court denied certiorari in the *Dorsey* case, a decision which in effect sanctioned Metropolitan Life Insurance Company's discrimination against Negroes in a large low-rent housing project constructed under New York State redevelopment law. The company received considerable aid from the state and city by means of special tax exemption; it was given land condemned through the state power of eminent domain; and the city maintained a degree of control over rent, profits, financing and altering of the structure. When the company refused to rent to Negroes an action was brought against it in the New York courts alleging "state action." The New York Supreme Court rejected the contention of state action, and the U.S. Supreme Court denied certiorari. *Ibid.*

"Because the United States Supreme Court since that time has handed down major decisions against discriminatory activity and has expanded the state-action concept, there is some question as to how the *Dorsey* case would be handled today. Nevertheless, with the uncertain status of the law concerning the equal-protection clause, the Fourteenth Amendment standing alone does not afford adequate protection." *Ibid.*

54. E. EHRLICH, FUNDAMENTAL PRINCIPLES OF THE SOCIOLOGY OF LAW 238 (1936).

capacity of rich and poor to realize the protections and benefits which the law provides.[55]

A number of illustrations of *de facto* bias can be given. In each case a law that is impartial on its face with respect to social class is biased in its effects.[56]

New York's highly restrictive divorce laws[57] are presumably applicable to all classes in society. In practice, however, they are more likely to prevent the poor than the rich from legally terminating their marriages, because poor people lack the resources to obtain out-of-state divorces. According to O'Gorman a "migratory divorce" is one means of evading the proscriptions of New York law, but he says:

> Since a migratory divorce is usually more expensive than one secured locally, this pattern of evasion is not equally open to all New Yorkers. If the state laws are easily avoided by financially independent residents, they can be avoided by others only at some sacrifice, and avoided not at all by those with low incomes. In this sense, the laws impinge differentially on the population; they are more binding on some groups than others.[58]

As a result the poor may resort to either a fraudulent New York action[59] or more commonly desertion. Equality might be achieved by restricting the freedom of the rich (*e.g.*, by New York's refusing to recognize the legality of certain out-of-state

---

55. According to Richard Lichtman, "Insofar as those human acts which the Constitution regards as rights are concerned the substantive end of justice is the creation of that situation most conducive to the equal self-realization of all the members of the community." He notes further that justice requires "the equal enjoyment of all institutions, privileges, advantages and conveniences created or regulated by law." R. Lichtman, *The Ethics of Compensatory Justice*, 1 LAW IN TRANS. Q. 76, 79, 85-86 (1964).

56. For some observations on *de facto* bias in procedural law as of the 1940's, see G. Olshausen, *Rich and Poor in Civil Procedure*, 11 SCIENCE AND SOCIETY 9 (1947). He considers certain provisional remedies (the temporary injunction, attachment, unlawful detainer and claim and delivery) and concludes that as a practical matter they are granted to the rich and denied to the poor. For example, the granting of a preliminary injunction is ordinarily conditioned upon the posting of a bond, and this tips the balance in favor of the litigant with means.

57. Until recently there were no grounds for divorce in New York except adultery. However, marriage could also be terminated through annulment proceedings and through an "Enoch Arden" decree which could be granted upon proof that one of the spouses had been absent for five years and was presumed dead. See H. O'GORMAN, LAWYERS AND MATRIMONIAL CASES: A STUDY OF INFORMAL PRESSURES IN PRIVATE PROFESSIONAL PRACTICE 11-13 (1963).

58. *Id.* at 22-23. See also *Id.* at 28 where it is reported that one of five lawyer informants objected to the New York divorce law because it discriminated against the poor.

59. *Id.* at 23. See also R. Wels, *New York: The Poor Man's Reno*, 35 CORNELL L.Q. 303-26 (1950).

divorces) [60] or by increasing the options of the poor (*e.g.*, by making New York divorces easier to obtain). [61]

Laws which specify the conditions under which legally enforceable bargains may be made are often implicitly biased against the poor. [62] George Brunn maintains that while an inequality of bargaining power underlies all transactions of buying and borrowing, the poor are especially disadvantaged. They lack the information, training, experience and economic resources to bargain on equal terms with sellers and lenders. [63] Thus the common law which embodies the *laissez faire* rule of the market place — let the buyer beware — is biased against the poor because they find it especially difficult to beware of abuses in the market place.

The draft law illustrates *de facto* bias in the law as we have defined it. Poor per-

---

60. A divorce can be granted in the state of domicile of either spouse, and full faith and credit requires that a legal divorce be recognized in all other states. However, another state can itself determine whether the spouse obtaining the decree was in fact domiciled in the state of divorce and refuse to recognize the divorce absent the requirement of domicile. See William v. North Carolina, 317 U.S. 387 (1942); 325 U.S. 226 (1945).

61. Wels maintains that a sense of the need for equality is one factor behind New York's permissive attitude toward fraudulent divorces. "If anything is basic in our nation and in our society, it is the concept that before the law all men are created equal, that all citizens shall receive equal treatment in our courts regardless of pocketbook or credit rating. It is, perhaps, a judicial awareness of the ease with which quick solutions to marital complexities are available to those able to pay for them, and a judicial sense of fairness, that has caused our judges to turn New York into a poor man's Reno for all with sufficiently elastic consciences. R. Wels, *supra* note 59, at 315. Since this article was written New York has made its divorce laws more permissive by adding new grounds. This will undoubtedly make it more possible for the poor to obtain divorces.

62. See D. CAPLOVITZ, *op. cit. supra* note 2, at 188. Note, *Project: Legislative Regulation of Retail Installment Financing*, 7 U.C.L.A. L. REV. 618, 750 (1960), observes that:
    A review of the California cases will quickly indicate that the retail buyer, knowing his rights and able to afford the cost of litigation, was adequately protected by the common law.
Clearly, this statement does not refer to the low-income buyer.

63. George Brunn believes that seller-buyer inequality has accelerated over the past century. With improvements in technology and the increasing complexity of credit practices, it is more difficult for the buyer to know what he is getting and on what terms. See Brunn, *supra* note 30, at 3-4; D. HAMILTON, THE CONSUMER IN OUR SOCIETY 331-34 (1962).

See also M. Brady, "The Consumer Speaks to the Research Experts," (paper presented at a Seminar on Research Needs in Consumer Economics, University of California, September 10, 1964). She observes that "the multiplication of the privileges of venders and lenders, their increasing resort to the power of the state, and their growing demands for public subsidy are taking place at a time *when technology has robbed the market place of its equalizer — the rational choice of informed consumers.*" *Id.* at 14 (emphasis added).

sons are less likely to have jobs which qualify them for deferment on occupational grounds, and they are less likely to be students. Moreover, they are less likely to know about the legal status of conscientious objectors and to be articulate enough to qualify for that status.[64]

Several tests are suggested for identifying and analyzing *de facto* bias; these may provide grounds for challenging the validity of laws that are biased in fact. (1) *Latent intent:* Where the real although hidden purpose of the law is to discriminate against the poor or other disadvantaged groups, this is a blatant case of *de facto* bias.[65] (2) *Knowledge of effect:* Where those responsible for making and enforcing the law are cognizant of its discriminatory effects but make no effort to reduce them, *de facto* bias is highlighted. (3) *Prior law as a contributing factor:* Where the barrier to equal protections or benefits is itself the result of prior laws there is a clear link between *de facto* and *de jure* bias. Kaplan contends that *de facto* segregation in schools may be unconstitutional as long as the segregated housing pattern resulted from state action (*e.g.*, "where a city council had by ordinance compelled Negroes to live in certain areas").[66] (4) *Egalitarian thrust of the law:* Where the law explicitly seeks to provide protections and benefits on an egalitarian basis, the failure to consider extra-legal obstacles to this end clearly subverts

---

64. For a discussion of bias in the draft law see D. Graham, J. Goodman and K. R. Johnson, *Draft Inequalities and Alternatives,* ATLANTIC MONTHLY 217 (February, 1966), 59-69. The statement regarding conscientious objector status is based on our field notes.

65. See tenBroek's discussion of Yick Wo v. Hopkins, 118 U.S. 356 (1886). He argues that the public had proceeded "with an evil eye and an unequal hand" because the real purpose of a San Francisco ordinance distinguishing between laundries in wooden buildings and those in brick and stone buildings was to drive the Chinese out of business. J. TEN-BROEK, EQUAL UNDER LAW 21-22 (enlarged ed. 1965).

66. Kaplan suggests that the Fourteenth Amendment cannot be enforced against private acts, but only against state action. See J. Kaplan, *Segregation Litigation and the Schools—Part II: The General Northern Problem,* 58 Nw. U. L. REV. 170, 212 (1963). Thus, the above reference to state action. For a counter-view, see L. Frantz, *Congressional Power to Enforce the Fourteenth Amendment Against Private Acts,* 73 YALE L.J. 1353 (1964). According to Frantz, "The theory that congressional power to enforce the Fourteenth Amendment can deal only with 'state action' will not stand up. It is obviously at odds with the original understanding. Even if we are not certain precisely what the original understanding was, we know that it could not have been this." *Id.* at 1381-82.

According to Robert Harris the majority of the members of the Thirty-ninth, Forty-second, and Forty-third Congresses believed that the equal protection clause did more than condemn official or state action. "They believed that it vested Congress at the very least with a primary power to set aside unequal state laws and a secondary power to afford protection to all persons in their enjoyment of constitutional rights when the states failed in their primary responsibility to do so either by neglecting to enact laws or by refusal or impotence to enforce them." *Id.* at 1381 n. 118.

the purpose of the law. In this situation there may be an affirmative duty to mitigate *de facto* bias.[67] (5) *Instrumental importance of the protection or benefit:* Where the inaccessible protection or benefit would be instrumental for the achievement of other legal rights and privileges, the discriminatory consequences of *de facto* bias are magnified. Thus, it is especially important to counter the incapacity of the poor to retain counsel.[68] Similarly it is more important to repeal a poll tax than a fishing tax. (6) *Relevance of barrier to legitimate purpose:* Where the poverty-relevant barrier to benefits can be shown to have a legitimate purpose, one can argue that the *de facto* bias in the law is justified. The more relevant the barrier is to a legitimate purpose, the more justified the barrier becomes.[69] Thus, if the purpose of barriers to voting is to achieve an informed electorate and if we assume this purpose to be legitimate, literacy tests become more justifiable than poll taxes.

A difficult question is how to distinguish between *de facto* bias and a failure to eliminate poverty. At some point the task of negating bias in the law becomes a task of changing the condition of the poor.[70] The complexity of the problem can

---

67. See R. Lichtman, *supra* note 55, at 83.

For a counter-view, see Justice Harlan's dissent in Douglas v. California, 372 U.S. 353, 361, 362 (1962), where he observes:

The States, of course, are prohibited by the Equal Protection Clause from discriminating between "rich" and "poor" *as such* in the formulation and application of their laws. But it is a far different thing to suggest that this provision prevents the State from adopting a law of general applicability that may affect the poor more harshly than it does the rich, or, on the other hand, from making some effort to redress economic imbalances while not eliminating them entirely. . . . (p. 361).

The State may have a moral obligation to eliminate the evils of poverty, but it is not required by the Equal Protection Clause to give to some whatever others can afford. (p. 362).

In Harlan's words the clause does not impose on the States an "affirmative duty to lift the handicaps flowing from differences in economic circumstances." *Ibid.* See also Justice Clark's dissent in the *Douglas* case, where he observes that "With this new fetish for indigency the court piles an intolerable burden on the State's judicial machinery." *Id.* at 359.

68. See White v. Maryland, 373 U.S. 59 (1963); Gideon v. Wainwright, 372 U.S. 335 (1963); Douglas v. California, 372 U.S. 353 (1963).

69. See J. tenBroek, *op. cit. supra* note 65, at 22-23. It is often difficult to determine the real purpose of biased laws because legislators themselves may believe their own rationalizations.

70. In considering the relevance of law for solving the consumer problems of the poor, Caplovitz addresses himself to a similar question:

In the final analysis, the consumer problems of low-income families cannot be divorced from the other problems facing them. Until society can find ways of raising their educational level, improving their occupational opportunities, in-be seen in the case of *de facto* segregation in schools, a problem combining poverty and race. Since *Brown v. Board of Education*[71] many have argued that Negroes have a right to be educated in integrated schools and that any law which establishes school boundaries in a manner that results in *de facto* segregation is a biased law.[72] Typical plans to end *de facto* segregation attempt to deal with the effects of segregated housing (*e.g.*, busing students across town); a more revolutionary approach might make housing patterns themselves the focus of concern. This would go further toward changing the condition of the poor.

REMEDIES

To counter and abate *de facto* bias, two approaches may be used: (1) *The poor may be given special benefits* to make the law work for them as it works for the rich. For example, they may be given free legal representation or the right to waive court costs. The barriers the rich overcome naturally are artificially removed from the poor. (2) *The rich may be penalized* as a means of equalizing benefits and protections. Thus, in most if not all small claims courts no one can have a lawyer. The practice of "reverse discrimination" combines the two approaches. Where the benefit is scarce, the special prerogatives given the disadvantaged may in effect penalize the advantaged. Giving Negroes temporary job

---

creasing their income, and reducing the discrimination against them — in short, until poverty itself is eradicated — only limited solutions to their problems as consumers can be found.

D. Caplovitz, *op. cit. supra* note 2, at 191-92.

71. 347 U.S. 483 (1954); 349 U.S. 294 (1955).

72. See, *e.g.*, Lichtman's statement that "children are denied equal protection of the law by the *fact* that they are segregated." He maintains that the intention behind the drawing of boundary lines is irrelevant. R. Lichtman, *supra* note 55, at 92. For a discussion of the contention that a constitutional violation is inherent in *de facto* segregation, see J. Kaplan *supra* note 66, at 211-14. For some further views, see A. Bickel, *Discrimination in Education* in DISCRIMINATION AND THE LAW 60-63, 70-77 (V. Countryman, ed. 1965).

In 1965 The Commonwealth of Massachusetts adopted "An Act for the Elimination of Racial Imbalance in the Public Schools." MASS. ANN. LAWS ch. 71, § 37C (1965). This was the first state to enact legislation aimed at eliminating *de facto* segregation in schools. The Act states in part: "It is hereby declared to be the policy of the Commonwealth to encourage all school committees to adopt as educational objectives the promotion of racial balance and the correction of existing racial imbalance in the public schools. The prevention or elimination of racial imbalance shall be an objective in all decisions involving the drawing or altering of school attendance lines and the selection of new school sites."

preference may be a means of achieving overall equality, but in the short run it penalizes whites.[73]

Because of their powerless position often the most effective remedies for the poor are those which allow a *collective* challenge of the status quo to combat institutionalized abuses which no single individual could effectively call into question. Thus, in the struggle for civil rights the mass demonstration has been an important tool for rallying public support and for welding the Negroes themselves into a politically effective movement.[74] In the struggle for decent housing the rent strike has at times been an effective means of holding landlords accountable.[75]

But a basic limitation of the law is its inability to treat the problems of the poor as essentially collective or class phenomena. The law has been slow to recognize and remedy the collective problems of slum tenants, low-income buyers and borrowers and public assistance recipients. And it has been slow to respond to the collective problems of Negroes in gaining full citizenship.[76]

Only recently, for example, has Congress acknowledged that such barriers to

---

73. Lichtman says that the "injury" to the white employee is not punishment, but the removal from an unfair advantage to which he is not entitled. R. Lichtman, *supra* note 55, at 98, 99.

74. We recognize that mass demonstrations do not always result in positive gains for Negroes or other disadvantaged groups in our society. Collective protests may alienate segments of the public and lead, temporarily at least, to repressive legislation. Furthermore, there is some reason to believe that the favorable legislation which has directly followed certain civil rights demonstrations, *e.g.*, the Voting Rights Bill which immediately followed the Selma protests, has been more a response to the violence of segregationists than to the collective expression of the Negro. See J. Howard, *The Provocation of Violence: A Civil Rights Tactic?*, 13 DISSENT 94 (1966).

75. According to Fossum, the rent strike is more a symptom than an effective device for bringing a lasting solution to the problems of slum housing. However, such strikes can and do dramatically indicate the problem that exists, and depending on the statutory framework in the jurisdictions in which they take place, they may be given legal sanction. In New York City which provides a favorable statutory framework for rent strikes, a high proportion of cases arising out of these actions have been decided in favor of the tenants. Thus, Fossum argues: "Where the technique has been given a statutory basis it serves both as a reasonably satisfactory channel for protesting an intolerable situation and as a substitute for the normal methods of code enforcement." J. Fossum, *Rent Withholding*, 53 CALIF. L. REV. 304, 323-25, 334-36 (1965).

76. Lawyers for the civil rights movement have consistently sought to file class suits for named plaintiffs suing to desegregate facilities "and for all others similarly situated," *i.e.*, for all other Negroes in the same community. But not all federal courts have recognized the validity of class actions on behalf of Negroes.

voting as literacy tests are obstacles that discriminate against Negroes collectively. The individualistic posture of the law appears to be changing. In a number of recent decisions federal courts have upheld the right of Negroes to engage in collective protest (marches, sit-ins, etc.),[77] in some instances sanctioning demonstrations which were alleged to disturb the peace or to violate trespassing laws. A further example is the court's decision in the *Button* case, which encourages the disadvantaged in general to band together in pursuing their legal interests.[78]

CONCLUSION

As we suggested above, the problem of remedying bias in the law shades into the problem of remedying poverty itself. Effecting *legal* equality becomes at some point a problem of effecting *social* equality. The effectiveness of law as an instrument for meeting the needs of the poor depends largely on its success in eliminating poverty, in moving the poor out of their deprived status. Today this is an important goal of law. It stems from an enlarged conception of the rights of man and a changing conception of the role of government in providing, protecting and implementing these rights. It also stems from the belief that poverty is caused by large impersonal forces in our complex industrial society, not by the poor themselves.[79] Reich argues that "when individuals have insufficient resources to live under conditions of health and decency, society has obligations to provide support, and the individual is entitled to that support as of right,"[80] and he adds that in our highly organized, institutional and bureaucratic society the avenue of providing basic rights to the poor must be through law.[81] What is involved here is a view of law as a positive,

---

77. See, *e.g.*, Cox v. Louisiana, 379 U.S. 536; U.S. 559 (1965); Hamm v. City of Rockhill, 379 U.S. 306 (1964); Bouie v. City of Columbia, 378 U.S. 347 (1964); Edwards v. South Carolina, 372 U.S. 229 (1962); Williams v. Wallace, 240 F. Supp. 100 (M.D. Ala. 1965). In the latter case concerning the march from Selma to Montgomery, the court issued an injunction restraining Alabama officials from "intimidating, threatening, coercing or interfering with" the proposed march, and the defendants were also enjoined from failing to provide adequate police protection to the plaintiffs in the exercise of their constitutional rights.

78. See Justice Brennan's statement for the Court in NAACP v. Button, 371 U.S. 415, 431 (1962). He suggests that "association for litigation may be the most effective form of political association" open to the Negro people. See A. Ginger, *Legal Processes: Litigation as a Form of Political Action*, in D. King and C. Quick, *op. cit. supra* note 52, at 195.

79. See C. Reich, *Individual Rights and Social Welfare: The Emerging Legal Issues*, 74 YALE L.J. 1245, 1255 (1965).

80. *Id.* at 1256.

81. *Ibid.*

affirmative force for change, not simply a reactive process. This approach is evidenced in such programs as medicare, the war on poverty, and voter registration for Negroes.[82]

Laws do not simply reflect the way men are treated in society; they influence the character of that treatment. When laws are biased against the interests of a particular group or class of people their deprived status is given official sanction. This is most obvious in the case of dual law, where the poor are officially relegated to a position of second-class citizenship. But favored party and *de facto* bias are perhaps even more pervasive and their impact more important. Thus, the law itself serves to define and maintain the position of the poor.[83]

ADMINISTRATION OF LAW AFFECTING THE POOR

The law is applied in a variety of agencies and settings, private as well as public, administrative as well as judicial. The study of agencies applying law to the poor directs attention to various conditions tending to undermine the integrity and effectiveness of these agencies. We shall first consider certain changes with respect to the structure and orientation of legal administration of special relevance to the poor, and the implications of these changes for the adjudicative functions of legal institutions. We shall then examine the way in which the inability of the poor to become effective constituents of legal agencies reinforces the reluctance of these institutions to serve the needs and interests of the poor.[84]

---

82. The affirmative programs of certain human relations commissions also appear relevant. Thus, the New York City commission has attempted to motivate banks and lending institutions to re-evaluate their operation "with an eye towards extending their mortgage financing services to members of minority groups," and it has attempted to motivate brokers, managers, and investors in housing to open all-white neighborhoods to minorities. J. Witherspoon, *Civil Rights Policy in the Federal System: Proposals for a Better Use of the Administrative Process*, 74 YALE L.J. 1171, 1209 (1965).

How effective those new programs will be in changing the relative economic position of the poor remains to be seen. Wilensky and Lebeaux observe that "the promise of the welfare state — minimum living standards brought about by government action to redistribute income and make opportunity equal — is nowhere fulfilled. . . . Up to the present in the United States . . . welfare programs have had small income-equalizing effect within the lower strata and a still smaller effect on the income distribution as a whole." H. WILENSKY & C. LEBEAUX, INDUSTRIAL SOCIETY AND SOCIAL WELFARE xii-xvi, 158-60 (1965).

83. In the view of Simmel and more recently Coser, poverty is a social category that emerges through societal definition: "The poor are men who have been so defined by society and have evoked particular reactions from it." See L. Coser, *The Sociology of Poverty*, 13 SOCIAL PROBLEMS 141 (1965).

84. Although we are more concerned with the administration of civil than criminal

SOCIETAL TRENDS

Increased Scale. Agencies involved in the administration of law have become large-scale enterprises. The population explosion in the metropolitan centers of the United States has led to an ever-increasing volume of cases processed through the courts and other agencies of government, necessitating an unprecedented expansion of facilities and manpower.[85] In Los Angeles County, for example, more than three times as many cases were filed in the trial courts in 1954 than in 1928.[86] Further, the lower the level of the judicial system, which means the more likely it will be dealing with the poor,[87] the greater the increase in case load.[88]

---

justice, reference will be made to the handling of criminal or quasi-criminal cases in lower-level courts. This is done partly because we are interested in presenting a general picture of inferior tribunals and because the distinction between a civil and criminal proceeding is often not meaningful at this level of the judicial system. Thus, the psychopathic and juvenile courts, although not formally criminal in nature, in fact make decisions that result in involuntary loss of liberty. Moreover, other courts and agencies handling civil matters involving the poor frequently employ essentially criminal sanctions in support of their decisions and actions. This is a prominent feature of courts dealing with consumer credit and family support. (With respect to the use of criminal process in the collection of civil debts in Pennsylvania, see Report of the Attorney General in the Investigation of the Magisterial System 29 [Department of Justice of Pennsylvania 1965]). We suspect, in fact, that there is a greater difference in the character of the proceeding between upper and lower-level courts than between civil and criminal proceedings within lower-level courts. Whether nominally civil or criminal, lower court proceedings appear to be essentially "administrative" in character.

85. M. Virtue, Survey of Metropolitan Courts 48 (1962).

86. J. Holbrook, A Survey of Metropolitan Trial Courts, Los Angeles Area 10, 14 (1956).

87. Although we know of no studies of the class background of litigants or parties in various civil tribunals, there is persuasive, albeit indirect evidence of the relation between court level and social class. Thus, the lower the level of the court in the judicial hierarchy: 1) the lower the jurisdictional amount of claims (which means the more likely it will be used by lower-class persons), 2) the less likely that parties will be represented by private counsel (reflecting in part the fewer economic resources of parties whose cases are processed through inferior tribunals, 3) the more likely that lawyers who deal with the court will have a low-status clientele. See J. Carlin, Lawyers' Ethics (1966), and 4) the more likely that the court will be processing types of cases reflecting problems that have a higher incidence in the lower than the upper classes. Thus, it is among the poor that we find the highest rates of family dissolution through divorce, separation or desertion (see W. Goode, *Family Disorganization,* in Contemporary Social Problems 416-28, R. Merton & R. Nisbet eds. 1961); mental illness (see B. Berelson & G. Steiner, Human Behavior: An Inventory of Scientific Findings 639, 1964); juvenile delinquency (see A. Cohen & J. Short, Jr., *Juvenile Delinquency,* in R. Merton & R. Nisbet, *op. cit. supra* at 87-88) and drunkenness (see D. Pittman & C. W. Gordon, Revolving Door

Within the judicial system this increase in volume of cases led initially to a "multiplicity of separate courts, with great overlap, duplication, waste, and confusion of jurisdiction."[89] It has been observed that this multiplicity of tribunals "seems to consist partly of duplicating general trial courts set up to ease congestion, and partly a piling up of separate, highly specialized courts."[90] These specialized dockets or courts — the family court, small claims court, psychopathic court, drunk court, juvenile court — process the bulk of cases involving the poor which come into the metropolitan judicial system; indeed, they were established mainly to accommodate the special problems of the urban poor.

A major consequence of magnified scale has been a tendency toward mass processing of cases. Especially in lower-level tribunals, cases are increasingly handled in a standardized mechanical manner, with little or no time allotted to any particular case and with little opportunity for examining or weighing facts or for exploring grounds for decisions.[91] The problems of scale are by no means

---

ch. 2, 1958). At any rate, these problems are most likely to come to the attention of public officials when they involve the poor.

The term "low-level" or "inferior" tribunal refers to local or state trial courts of limited or special jurisdiction (including the family, drunk, psychopathic, small claims and juvenile courts) as opposed to state trial courts of general jurisdiction and appellate courts. Court level is usually correlated with the salary and tenure of judges and their educational background and experience. See J. Carlin, *supra* at ch. 5. It is interesting to note that in California, which has a consolidated court system, assignments to those departments in the Superior Court that correspond to low-level courts in other states (such as juvenile or domestic relations) are generally designated as the least desirable by judges.

88. The largest increase in the number of filings between 1928 and 1954 was found in the small claims, domestic relations, juvenile, traffic and psychopathic courts. The smallest increase took place with respect to other civil cases; in fact, there was a 36% decline in the number of these cases filed in the Superior Court. See J. Holbrook, *op. cit. supra* note 86.

89. M. Virtue, *op. cit, supra* note 85, at 136. See also D. Peck, *Court Organization and Procedures to Meet the Needs of Modern Society*, 33 Ind. L.J. 182-197 (1958).

90. M. Virtue, *op. cit. supra* note 85, at 157.

91. Holbrook reports that the drunk court in Los Angeles processes between 200 and 250 cases a day. J. Holbrook, *op. cit. supra* note 86, at 317.

This is also clearly evident in the following account drawn from our field notes, of the processing of public drunkenness cases in the Municipal Court of San Francisco:

The bailiffs bring in the defendants from the jail in groups of about 20. The men stand in two lines behind a three-foot high horizontal bar which separates the defendants from the rest of the courtroom. After the defendants have filed into the court the judge repeats the following rubric: "You men are all charged with being publicly drunk. Do any of you plead not guilty?" (The judge pauses about five

limited to the courts but may be seen also in other agencies of law administration. Thus, case loads in welfare agencies and probation departments may attain similar magnitudes as in drunk, juvenile and domestic relations courts, with similar pressures toward mass processing.

New Tasks. One of the characteristic features of our society is the steadily expanding scope of government. With the weakening of kinship and other traditional social units large scale formal organizations, both public and private, are called upon to perform tasks and satisfy needs that previously had been taken care of in less formal ways.[92] The development is particularly evident in the expansion of governmental activity on behalf of the poor. This may be seen in the extension of health, education and welfare benefits through social security and welfare legislation, medicare and aid to education — and in the passage of the Economic Opportunity Act.

Along with the establishment of agencies to implement these various programs there has developed a need for insuring fairness and reasonableness, particularly in the exercise of the adjudicative or quasi-adjudicative functions of these organizations. Decisions regarding eligibility for benefits represent an important although by no means the only area of concern.

The expanded scope of the legal system is also reflected in the assumption of administrative tasks by nominally judicial agencies. Thus, to an increasing extent,

---

seconds to see if there are any "not guilty" pleas.) "All guilty. Answer to your name as it is called." The men are arranged by the bailiff in the line in the order in which their name will be called for sentencing.

Domestic relations (principally family support) cases are usually disposed of in summary fashion under the ever present pressure for dispatch:

When one case was called there was no reply and the judge said, "Passed" immediately. The clerk began to explain something, but was interrupted angrily by the judge who said, "Passed, passed. Call the next one quickly." In one third of all cases heard, a positive reference was made by the judge for a need to hurry.

Drawn from our field notes.

Mass processing is also a characteristic feature of juvenile and commitment proceedings and uncontested divorce actions. A judge in Santa Clara County summed up the situation in this way:

All one can think of any longer is getting through the mill; the court becomes a treadmill and not a forum for adjudication.

Drawn from our field notes.

92. See P. Selznick, *Legal Institutions and Social Controls,* 17 VAND. L. REV. 79-90 (1963).

courts serving the poor seem to define their principal objective as the solution of a social problem by a benevolent administrator rather than the resolution of a legal dispute by an impartial adjudicator.[93] The orientation of such courts has been characterized as "individualized justice"; decisions are tailored to who the person is rather than to what he has done.[94] This concern for the person, and more particularly for the rehabilitation of the disadvantaged, entails a conception of the poor as having problems rather than grievances and of needing treatment not

93. The County Court of Philadelphia, for example, in its 47th Annual Report, asserts that its domestic relations court is guided by:

the modern idea of a family court which has as its aim the coordination of the handling of all family problems in one agency, and the utilization of social skills and modern methods for the re-establishment and strengthening of families. . . . From the outset the work of the domestic relations division in the new court was concerned with the problem of integration of family life, rather than with the strictly legal issues as to whether the family ties should be severed . . . or whether the husband had a duty to support the family members.

County Court of Philadelphia, Forty-Seventh Annual Report 195-96 (1960).

A focus on "problem solving" is also evident in the philosophy of the Juvenile Court. According to the Philadelphia report:

The welfare of the child is the guiding principle of operation in the Juvenile Division of the Municipal Court of Philadelphia. . . . The purpose of the Juvenile court law has been defined by the Supreme Court of Pennsylvania as being the "salvation of children" rather than the punishment of offenders (Commonwealth v. Fisher, 213 Pa. 48). It is the characteristics of the child and of his family more than the nature of his delinquent conduct which governs the dispositions of juvenile courts. Id. at 9, 10, 11.

94. See G. L. Schramm, *Philosophy of the Juvenile Court*, 261 Annals 101 (1949). David Matza contends: "Individualized justice is the basic precept in the philosophy of the juvenile court. More generally, it is commended to all officials who deal with juveniles. We should, it is suggested by enlightened professionals, gear our official dispositions to suit the individual needs of the accused rather than respond in an automatic fashion to the offense he has allegedly committed. The relating of disposition to individual needs instead of to the offense is a central aspect of the treatment viewpoint." D. Matza, Delinquency and Drift 111-12 (1964).

Maxine Virtue notes that a redefinition of goals was well underway by the twenties:

[T]he movement towards individualized justice raised questions concerning the role of the judge as an adjuster of personal relations and a rehabilitator of the socially disadvantaged as well as, or perhaps in place of, a decider of conflicts presented through the adversary process alone. . . . [T]here was by that time (the late twenties) a developing trend to encourage benign and even therapeutic handling of juvenile cases, and to tolerate the beginnings of a trend towards development of specialized courts, such as family courts, staffed by judges with sympathy and special knowledge of such cases and by administrative aides with various skills for diagnosing and solving litigants' problems.

M. Virtue, *op. cit. supra* note 85, at 115.

justice. More fundamentally, however, it reflects an image of the poor as essentially incompetent, as incapable of knowing their interests or asserting them.[95]

Not only are the poor assumed to be incompetent and treated, in effect, as wards of the court, but there is a further assumption of an essential harmony of interests between the poor citizen and the state.[96] Accordingly the task of the court is not to arrive at a determination with respect to conflicting rights, but to restore and promote social equilibrium, to heal and to cure. Indeed, the failure of parties to realize their common interests is a prime indication of their need for help. As in the therapeutic situation, stated complaints and grievances are merely the starting points for a more fundamental analysis; they are not to be taken at face value.[97]

Given these assumptions by the court the notion of a contest between adverse interests is deplored, formal rules of evidence and procedure are avoided, and the services of counsel discouraged. The traditional model of adjudication is viewed as irrelevant to, if not preventing, a solution in the best interest of the "client."[98]

---

95. It is perhaps no accident that the treatment orientation first appeared in the juvenile court, since the youthful character of its clientele made more justifiable the assumption of incompetence.

The striking parallel between the orientation of Soviet courts and our lower-level tribunals is explicitly noted by Harold J. Berman:

> As the atmosphere of the Soviet criminal trial approximates that of our juvenile courts, so the atmosphere of a Soviet civil suit may perhaps bear an analogy to that of our domestic relations courts.

H. BERMAN, JUSTICE IN THE U.S.S.R. 309 (1963). The author also notes that Soviet judges "play the part of a parent or guardian: Indeed the whole legal system is parental." *Id.* at 754.

96. With respect to the juvenile court it has been observed: "The delinquent . . . is not (conceived as) the enemy of society. He is society's child, and therefore the interests of the state and the child do not conflict but coincide." J. Handler, *The Juvenile Court and the Adversary System: Problems of Function and Form*, 1965 WIS. L. REV. 10 (1965).

97. Note the following observation in connection with commitment proceedings:

> In another case, the physician stated that he thought the patient was suspicious and distrustful because he asked about the possibility of being represented by counsel at the judicial hearing.

T. Scheff, *Societal Reaction to Deviance*, 11 SOCIAL PROBLEMS 409 (1964).

98. This orientation is clearly evident in the following comment of a family counsellor in a conciliation court:

> Ideally, attorneys should not be in the court as they often inflame parties and produce tension and create the atmosphere of a court case involving one person against another, rather than the ideal atmosphere of a hearing which is in the interests of both parties.

An increasing emphasis on rehabilitation may also be noted in certain welfare agencies, with similar consequences for the legal rights of the poor citizen. Recipients of these agencies are seen as reservoirs of a great many "needs," only one of which may be the need for financial assistance. Medical care or psychiatric help may be required; recipients may need education or job training; instruction may be called for in managing a budget, in cleaning up an apartment, in child training practices. The list is perhaps endless, depending as it does on the agency officials' views of what is required for effective family functioning. Public assistance law is perceived by this "new style" agency as providing a mandate for "serving" these needs.[99] Armed with this mandate agency officials become social therapists.

If the distinctive marks of the old-style agency were suspiciousness and harshness, the new-style agency is characterized by a certainty that the professionals who work for the agency know what the client "needs." And with this certainty may come a greater intrusiveness, one that looks beyond qualifications for assistance to the possibility of changing the moral character of recipients in order to render them whole and competent to deal with their life situation. To do this the new-style agent must find ways to diagnose the social and psychological defects of the poor; this obviously requires wide access to, as well as scrutiny of, the personal and private lives of his clients.

The potential danger of the new-style agency is that it may become a tool for total governmental control. The law would then provide a license for regulating the detailed life activities of those citizens "eligible" for such direction. It might well legitimize the reach of government into every circumstance that might bear

---

Drawn from our field notes.

Further indication of the hostility of the court toward a formal adjudicative proceeding may be seen in the following observation:

> On one occasion when he (the judge in a domestic relations department) granted the petition of wife's counsel that husband be restrained from removing the child from the state on a visit, this attorney said: "I would like to offer points and authorities, Your Honor." "I don't want to hear any points and authorities," was the judge's response, "I'm not interested in the mere legalistics of the matter."

Ibid.

99. See, *e.g.*, CAL. WELFARE & INST'NS CODE § 19: "Due regard for the preservation of family life, and . . . to encourage self-respect, self-reliance, and the desire to be a good citizen, useful to society." (Language omitted in 1965 amendment.) Cited in J. tenBroek, *supra* note 39, at 678. The very language of the Code, however, might well have been fashioned into tools of legal argument to restrain and limit official action, particularly insofar as such action tends to denigrate recipients and weaken their self-respect.

on the process of rehabilitation. Traditional guarantees of procedural due process would be seen as unnecessary — indeed as interfering with certain commonly desired therapeutic goals. Attorneys would become irrelevant; client dissent a sign that more therapy was called for. Judicial review of agency decisions would be unneccessary; judges would wonder what their role could possibly be beyond placing a ritual stamp of approval on decisions made for reasons best understood by others. A citizen who qualified for this benign control might be stripped of his right to mean what he said, which is perhaps the most fundamental right of all. Although we have not yet reached such a pass, the tendency is clear enough. As sociologists we are led to explore the forces moving the legal system toward total control and the forces which counterbalance and counteract this movement.

IMPLICATIONS FOR THE ADJUDICATIVE PROCESS

As we have already suggested, a major consequence of the increased scale and expanded scope of the legal system is a tendency for the adjudicative process to be undermined, particularly in lower-level courts and agencies. In juvenile and family courts, in welfare agencies and commitment proceedings, decisions affecting the legal rights of the poor are usually not based upon reasoned argument or a determinate set of rules, and there is little concern for preserving or establishing procedures for safeguarding individual rights.

Weakening of Procedural Standards. Failure to give proper notice to parties appears to be a common practice in many lower-level tribunals.[100] Lack of notice obviously deprives the affected party of an opportunity to be heard. Even when the person is present he still may be effectively denied meaningful participation in the proceeding.[101]

---

100. A study of commitment procedures in New York State reports:

Although Section 74 (most patients come to state mental hospital under this Section of the New York Mental Hygiene Law) contemplates notice to the patient and a hearing before the court order for the original admission, in practice . . . notice is usually not given and a hearing is held in only a minority of cases.

ASSN. OF THE BAR OF THE CITY OF NEW YORK, MENTAL ILLNESS AND DUE PROCESS 108 (1962).

101. Thus, in a report of a study conducted in Wisconsin it was noted:

In one urban court (the court with the largest number of cases) the only contact between the judge and the patient was in a preliminary hearing. This hearing was held with such lightning rapidity (1.6 minutes average) and followed such a standard and unvarying format that it was obvious that the judge made no attempt to use the hearing results in arriving at a decision.

The opportunity to challenge or rebut the information upon which decisions are made is frequently very limited. Although in lower court decisions considerable weight is attached to the reports of probation officers, family service workers, psychiatrists and others, these reports may not be offered in evidence, and even when they are those who have prepared them are usually not available for cross-examination.[102]

In many lower level tribunals rules of evidence are either explicitly eliminated or are virtually unobserved in practice.[103] Weakening the rules of evidence increases the likelihood that decisions will rest on something less than competent testimony. Moreover the burden frequently falls on the defendant to prove his "innocence" or the absence of liability.[104] An important consequence is the eliciting of self-incriminating testimony. Although adolescents generally have a right not

---

He asked three questions uniformly: "How are you feeling?", "How are you being treated?", and "If the doctors recommend that you stay here a while, would you cooperate?" No matter how the patient responded, the judge immediately signified that the hearing was over, cutting off some of the patients in the middle of a sentence.

Thomas Scheff, *Social Conditions for Rationality,* 7 AM. BEHAV. SCIEN. 22 (1964). See also, MENTAL ILLNESS AND DUE PROCESS, *op. cit. supra* note 100, at 19.

102. In the Children's Court in New York City it has been observed:

It was left free to the individual judge to decide how much of the social history would be reviewed prior to the decision, but one study indicated that at least seventy-five per cent of the judges examined the histories prior to a determination of jurisdiction. There was little or no opportunity for respondents to challenge the information in their histories. In not one observed case was there an objection to any testimony. . . .

J. Handler, *supra* note 96, at 22-23.

103. In a study of Los Angeles courts it was noted with respect to commitment cases: "No attention is paid to the formal rules of evidence." J. Holbrook, *op. cit. supra* note 86, at 244. With respect to the juvenile court it was noted:

Rules of evidence are not adhered to; the court desires to get all the facts without being bound by confining rules. . . . The language used is simple and geared to the child's understanding. For example, "It says here that you took a quart of oil from Mr. Brown. Is that true, John?"

Id. at 238.

104. Thus, Thomas Scheff observes:

The fact that courts seldom release patients, and the perfunctory manner in which the legal and medical procedures are carried out, suggest that the judicial decision to retain patients in the hospital for treatment is routine and largely based on the presumption of illness.

T. Scheff, *supra* note 97, at 411.

to testify in juvenile court it has been shown in California, for example, that "some courts unfortunately take coercive action when a child refuses to testify."[105]

A further indication of the reduction of procedural safeguards is the characteristic absence of attorneys from lower level tribunals and agencies. In the Children's Court in New York City, for example, 92 per cent of all respondents during 1959 were not represented by counsel;[106] Holbrook reports that at the time of his study 95 per cent of juveniles in Los Angeles did not have counsel. In commitment proceedings lawyers appeared in only 7 per cent of cases processed by the County Court in Los Angeles.[107] Equally low figures are reported for drunk cases and arraignment of non-traffic misdemeanor cases.[108] Where a party has a right to counsel he is frequently discouraged from exercising it.[109]

Without the assistance of competent counsel parties may be effectively denied the opportunity to challenge the findings and decisions of the court or to insist on other procedural safeguards. Lack of counsel undoubtedly accounts for the largely pro forma character of most proceedings in lower-level tribunals.

Control over judicial proceedings in lower-level tribunals through appellate review is virtually absent. In 1959-60, out of nearly 20,000 adolescents adjudged delinquent or neglected in New York City only 4 cases were appealed.[110] This is apparently also the pattern for civil proceedings involving the poor.

Reduction of Adversariness. Although court cases at all levels of the judicial system are generally disposed of in a non-adversarial manner, this is more likely to be the case in those tribunals that deal with the poor. Thus, only 5 per cent of all dispositions in the Municipal Court in California in 1962 involved a formally contested trial (both sides presenting evidence in a hearing), compared with 10 per cent of all Superior Court dispositions and 12 per cent of all civil cases in the Superior Court.[111]

---

105. J. Handler, *supra* note 96, at 33.

106. C. Schinitsky, *The Role of the Lawyer in Children's Court*, 17 RECORD OF N.Y.C.B.A. 10 (1962). It should be noted that the Family Court Act of 1963 may have increased the use of attorneys in juvenile cases.

107. J. Holbrook, *op. cit. supra* note 86, at 78.

108. *Ibid.*

109. Maxine Virtue notes that in mental and juvenile cases "members of court staffs actively discourage litigants from seeking counsel." M. Virtue, *op. cit. supra* note 85, at 299.

110. J. Handler, *supra* note 96, at 22.

111. JUDICIAL COUNCIL OF CALIFORNIA, 1962 ANNUAL REPORT 151 (1963).

The weakening of the adversary system in civil as well as in criminal cases is partly a reflection of the increasingly large volume of cases processed through inferior tribunals and the resultant pressures for more efficient procedures. This may account for the hostile reaction of many judges, particularly in traffic courts, to demands for a formal hearing.[112]

The reduction of adversariness is also a function of the increasing emphasis on diagnosis and treatment by non-legal personnel. This is most evident in the juvenile and family courts and in commitment of the mentally ill.[113]

The reduction of adversariness has at least three important effects on the character of the proceedings. First, it very likely hinders the accurate determination of facts. Reliance solely on the court for developing and presenting the facts may restrict information and encourage a premature labeling of the case "to try to fit it into a familiar pattern in an effort to order the mass of facts around a tentative theory."[114] An adversary presentation, "hearing both sides of the story," tends to facilitate the exploration and sifting of facts and provides some assurance against pre-judgment and partiality. Second, a non-adversary proceeding probably increases the reliance of the court on the arguments and testimony of the party having the greater resources for developing his case; this is particularly likely when one of the parties is an agency of government. An adversary proceeding on the other hand tends to place the parties on a more equal footing. Finally, the reduction of adversariness limits the opportunity of parties to challenge the bases of the court's actions and decisions and increases the burden on the court for using self-restraint in the exercise of its powers.

Abdication of Responsibility. In the many specialized tribunals it has become common practice for judges to delegate authority for decision-making to administrative personnel: probation officers, medical examiners, marriage counsellors, referees, commissioners and others. According to Maxine Virtue these personnel have, to an increasing extent,

> taken over activities usually regarded as judicial in response to the tremendous needs and pressures of the metropolitan caseload. Sometimes, as where a commissioner assembles information or works out a solution under judicial supervision, this seemed a legitimate method of stretching the judge's reach. Sometimes, as where juvenile court personnel administratively designated "referees" dispose of all cases falling within a certain classification without any real judicial super-

---

112. M. Virtue, *op. cit. supra* note 85, at 349.
113. *Id.* at 221, and J. Handler, *supra* note 96, at 26.
114. *Id.* at 30.

vision, it seemed a usurpation of the judicial function by personnel untrained in legal disciplines and unaware of the indispensability of due process.[115]

This delegation of judicial authority often results, in effect, in shifting the responsibility for making decisions; the judge does little more than rubber-stamp the decisions of others.[116]

Meaningful review of decisions made by non-judicial personnel is important because: (1) the consequences of such decisions are often punitive, (2) the "expert" determination is frequently routine and perfunctory,[117] and (3) the affected party has little opportunity for effective participation in the "preliminary hearing" conducted by non-judicial personnel.[118] He cannot readily present testi-

---

115. M. Virtue, *op. cit. supra* note 85, at 209. See also M. VIRTUE, SURVEY OF METRO-POLITAN COURTS DETROIT AREA, 102, 103, 105 (1950); J. Handler, *supra* note 96, at 11; Holbrook *op. cit. supra* note 86, at 155.

116. *Mental Illness and Due Process, op. cit. supra* note 100, at 5, 194. See also J. Handler, *supra* note 96, at 17. In our interviews with judges the same picture appears:

> In most [juvenile] cases, after all, the judge follows the recommendation of the probation officer. Actually we act as rubber stamps, and I don't know how it could be otherwise.
>
> Interviewer: You mean you feel superfluous?
>
> Judge: Yes, most of the time.

Drawn from our field notes.

117. Certificates (for involuntary commitment) are signed as a matter of course by staff physicians . . . after little or no examination. . . . The so-called examinations are made on an assembly line basis, often being completed in two or three minutes, and never taking more than ten minutes. Although psychiatrists agree that it is practically impossible to determine a person's sanity on the basis of such a short and hurried interview, doctors . . . recommend confinement in 77% of the cases.

L. Kutner, *The Illusion of Due Process in Commitment Proceedings,* 57 Nw. U.L. REV. 383 (1962). One reason for the perfunctory character of the medical examination is indicated by the following comment of a court-appointed psychiatrist: "It's not remunerative. I'm taking a hell of a cut. I can't spend 45 minutes with a patient. I don't have the time. It doesn't pay." T. Scheff, *supra* note 101. With respect to juvenile cases, it has been noted:

> The case load [of probation officers in the Los Angeles Juvenile Court] is so heavy at the present time (one probation officer to every eighty-five children) that the probation officer may see the child only once before the regular hearing.

J. Holbrook, *op. cit. supra* note 86, at 338.

118. It is said that these (probation) officers are even less interested than the judges in proving specific conduct; their attitude is to avoid "legal technicalities" which may slow or prevent the application of what they think is needed therapy . . .

mony or challenge the determination of the presiding or examining officer. However, given the pressures created by the large volume of cases that are finally brought to the court, the absence of clear standards for the decisions of "experts" and the lack of counsel, there is little opportunity for effective review of these precourt determinations. Thus, in these specialized tribunals delegation of responsibility for decisions seems to permit if not openly encourage unfettered official discretion.

Diffusion of Responsibility. With the increasing bureaucratization of legal institutions and the greater reliance placed on the judgments of administrative personnel, there has been a tendency to fragment responsibility for authoritative decision-making. Under these conditions it becomes difficult to determine when, on what grounds and by whom such decisions have been made. Diffusion of responsibility occurs both within and between various lower-level agencies.

Determinations regarding initial and continuing eligibility for public assistance may involve not only intake workers but case workers, supervisors and support investigators.[119] An important consequence is that the grounds for an adverse determination, and the information upon which it is based, are often hidden from view.[120] According to the Moreland Commission Report: "In one county, for example, 37.5 per cent of those interviewed claimed they were not told why assistance was cut off, and the case records failed to indicate that the former recipient had been given a reason."[121] Sparer observes:

> The same type of objections apply, but more forcefully, to the regulatory practices of station adjustment or unofficial delinquency. There is no legal authority for this practice and there are no controls unless the adolescent or their parents have the temerity to challenge the officer. In view of the type of persons brought before the police, the power relationships, and even the threats to send adolescents to court if they do not comply, such challenges would be exceedingly unlikely.

J. Handler, *supra* note 96, at 18.

119. See REPORT TO THE MORELAND COMMISSION ON WELFARE OF FINDINGS OF THE STUDY OF THE PUBLIC ASSISTANCE PROGRAM AND OPERATIONS OF THE STATE OF NEW YORK 46, 49 (1962).

120. See, *e.g.*, J. Witherspoon, *supra* note 82, at 1197. The author notes:
> the commissions do not disclose the particular data which provide the basis for their determination of probable cause. Until the legal criteria underlying the concept of probable cause are expounded and the particular data to which they are applied made available and studied, it will not be possible to judge the correctness of commissions' determinations.

Id. at 1198.

121. PUBLIC WELFARE IN THE STATE OF NEW YORK, 68 (1963).

> At times, a family suspended from welfare assistance because of wrongdoing or fraud cannot, even with the aid of private social workers, obtain the precise nature and ground for the suspension. Without the right to acquire this information and confront his accusers, the client is effectively precluded from disproving the charge.[122]

Diffusion of responsibility for decision-making also results from the overlapping of jurisdiction and control among various lower-level courts and agencies.

A recent study in California indicates the extent to which the functions of welfare agencies overlap those of various judicial and law enforcement agencies. In discussing the relation between welfare and the probation department of the juvenile court in handling dependent and neglected children, it was noted:

> There is no basic statewide delineation of functions. Responsibility for service varies from county to county. Frequently, both welfare departments and probation departments give service to the same family.

> When the child is not made a dependent child or ward of the court, casework service is usually provided by the county welfare department or by a private agency in the community. But there are exceptions. The probation departments in some counties carry a sizeable load of "informal" probation cases.[123]

Similar overlap was found in the relation between welfare and the district attorney's office in determining the whereabouts and financial status of the absent parent and in investigating alleged fraud on the part of welfare recipients.[124]

INEFFECTIVE CONSTITUENCIES

Study of law and poverty underscores the fact that the administration of justice is affected by the structure of political and economic power. From the sociological perspective the principal task is to explore the ways in which these forces shape the character of legal agencies. The major policy question, particularly from the point of view of those committed to the defense of legal values, may be put in this way: What are the institutional arrangements that will insure that the balance of influence will on the one hand provide agencies of justice with adequate legal resources, and on the other hand permit them to proceed in a reasoned, unbiased and effective fashion?

---

122. E. Sparer, *The Role of the Welfare Client's Lawyer*, 12 U.C.L.A. L. Rev. 361, 372 (1965).

123. I. Reichert, Jr. "A Report on Relationships Between Welfare and Law Enforcement Agencies in California" 52, unpublished report, 1962.

124. *Id.* at 34.

The poor are generally ineffective constituents of legal institutions, including those specifically designed to serve their interests. They rarely have the motivation or capacity for using legal agencies to their own advantage or for exerting pressures on agencies to remain true to statutory objectives. Consequently, these agencies tend to remain unresponsive if not indifferent to the special needs of the poor; they are frequently reluctant either to enlarge their resources or to play a more active role in implementing their purported policies, which include the enforcement and protection of the legal rights of the poor. Let us now consider in more detail these limitations in the character and operation of agencies dealing with the poor.

Captivity. Agencies serving the poor tend to become captives of interests alien to if not conflicting with those of the poor. Thus, although welfare agencies are charged with providing care and support for the needy, they frequently follow a restrictive, punitive policy of welfare administration.[125] These practices stem in part from the responsiveness of welfare officials to those segments of the community that would penalize the poor and deter them from seeking aid.[126] A principal concern is for minimizing burdens on the public purse; and administrators become highly sensitive to community attitudes of outrage and alarm over alleged evidence of chiseling and waste.[127]

---

125. Report to the Moreland Commission, *op. cit. supra* note 119, at 3.
126. The following has been suggested as a possible explanation:

> The simple fact is that the vast majority of us, in the comfortable prosperity of our affluent society, do not approve of the poor. . . . (We) have set up every kind of barrier to exclude or discourage the desperately poor from even (a minimal) level of aid: arbitrary definitions of eligibility related to age, family relationship (such as the absurd requirement in many states that there be no man in the home), employability, duration of residence in the state, and every sort of procedural hurdle and humiliation.

E. Wickenden, "Administration of Welfare Rights" 2-3, 4, paper presented at the National Conference on Law and Poverty, Washington, D.C., June, 1965.

127. According to a poll conducted by the Moreland Commission of people of voting age throughout New York State:

> Virtually one-third of the New Yorkers questioned said that they believed 40 per cent or more of all relief recipients were chiseling "in one way or another." Close to another one-third believed that chiseling ranged between 11 per cent and 39 per cent of those on relief rolls. These private and personal estimates were far beyond what even the most caustic critics of public welfare claimed in print or in open meetings. They were, of course, ill-informed guesses — far from the facts of the matter, or at least far from the best available estimates.

Report to the Moreland Commission, *supra* note 119, at 11.

Pressures from the legislature and the public for strict accountability of money spent contribute to an immense proliferation of administrative rules and regulations relative to the decisions of public assistance workers and a corresponding increase in paper work which further restricts the capacity of welfare agencies to serve the needs of their poor clients. The burdens imposed by this "paperwork explosion" are critically noted in the Moreland Commission Report:

> "From my own experience and research," said one witness at our public hearing, "50 to 60 per cent of a caseworker's time is spent on bookkeeping. I thought I would be able to help people, but I was a bookkeeper." He related an instance in which an elderly couple — each getting Old Age Assistance, and each treated as a separate case — moved to a new neighborhood and the rent went up. To revise the rent allowance upward, the witness said, he had to fill out and file 30 different pieces of paper. This paperwork explosion plagues welfare workers everywhere. . . . The files bulge with records — in triplicate, quadruplicate and quintuplicate — all designed to set forth facts and to substantiate action and justify reimbursement. Accountability is necessary. But at what point does filling out forms pass the point of diminishing returns, and become record keeping simply for the purpose of record keeping? At what point does desk work become so demanding that social workers have little time to serve the needy and the dependent?[128]

Perhaps a more striking instance of captivity is illustrated by the fate of at least one Small Claims Court. In the view of its founders and supporters this specialized tribunal was created to provide a forum in which the poor plaintiff, unhindered by legal technicalities and prohibitive court costs, would be able to pursue his legal rights and remedies. The data indicate, however, that the court has been captured by business interests who find it a useful tool in the collection of debts against the poor. A recent study of the Oakland-Piedmont Small Claims Court showed that two out of three users were either business firms (jewelry and department stores, mail order houses, finance companies) or, to a lesser extent, local government agencies (principally the County of Alameda with claims for hospital services rendered and for unpaid taxes). Most (85 per cent) of these organization plaintiffs filed several claims at a time, and most were frequent users of the court.[129] It is, thus, principally the business community, not the poor, that reaps the advantage of this inexpensive and speedy process. Moreover, the lawyer-less procedure gives the business concern the opportunity to oppose an unskilled and inexperienced poor person with a trained, experienced agent. (More than 85 per cent of the defendants

---

128. *Id.* at 76.

129. C. Pragter, R. McCloskey & M. Reinis, *The California Small Claims Court* 40, 45, 55, student paper, University of California, 1963, subsequently published in condensed form in 52 CALIF. L. REV. 876 (1964).

in the Oakland-Piedmont Small Claims Court were individuals; the remainder were businesses or government agencies.) The trend throughout the United States is toward increased use of the small claims procedure for collection purposes.[130]

The tendency of certain tribunals to surrender to the interests of their business users may account for the apparent failure to provide defendants with certain procedural safeguards. Lack of notice is said to be common, and it is alleged to be one of the principal reasons for the very high proportion of default judgments in collections and landlord-tenant cases.[131] The hopeless position of the poor defend-

---

130. Collection agents and professional men employ the Small Claims Court's facilities in increasing number. However, no serious objection has been raised to this tendency; in fact, two states . . . have deleted from their statutes a limitation on the number of claims which an individual may bring before the court during a particular week or month. This action would seem to encourage the use of small claims courts by repeating claimants as well as by the occasional litigant.

Id. at 29.

131. A recent study of the Magistrate's Court in Philadelphia documents this phenomenon:

When the unsworn testimony of the magistrates was taken, it was readily apparent that many of the magistrates did not know any of the legal requirements for service. Some even thought that civil summons could be mailed. Moreover, constables are required by law to file a return of service stating the precise manner in which service was made. This return is the only evidence available to the magistrate to enable him to decide whether he has jurisdiction over the person of the defendant. Nevertheless, in one court no returns of service are made. In other courts, where thousands of returns of service were examined by Justice Investigators, it was found that hundreds of returns were defective on their face, and in all those cases the magistrate had proceeded to give judgments by default.

In some cases judgments were entered even though the constable's return stated affirmatively that he had been unable to make service at all. When confronted with examples of improper service, the magistrates generally indicated that this is a matter for the constable to correct since the magistrates assume that the constable does his job properly. Such an assumption is not only factually unfounded, but amounts to an abrogation of the magistrates' fundamental duty. . . . Frequently a defendant's first knowledge of the claim is obtained when he receives a constable's notice of levy upon his household goods or when his neighbors read of the constable's sale notice in the newspaper.

REPORT OF THE ATTORNEY GENERAL ON THE INVESTIGATION OF THE MAGISTERIAL SYSTEM 30 (Department of Justice, Commonwealth of Pennsylvania, 1965).

Similar practices are reported with respect to the landlord-tenant court in New York City. See N. LeBlanc, *Landlord-Tenant Problems*, in THE EXTENSION OF LEGAL SERVICES TO THE POOR 52-53 (U.S. Dept. of HEW, 1964).

ant in such cases is "strikingly illustrated by the fact that the dockets now being used [in the Magistrate's Court of Philadelphia] . . . do not even have a space for the entry of [a judgment for the defendant]."[132]

The report on the Magistrate's Court in Philadelphia suggests a more extreme form of captivity in the direct pecuniary interest of court personnel in the outcome of collection proceedings.[133] Magistrates themselves may share in the recoveries they award;[134] they may also take an active part in seeking to collect claims before trial.[135]

It is rarely the case that an agency serving the poor will attempt to mobilize its potential clients into an effective constituency. A singular exception is found in the expressed policy of the Economic Opportunity Act of 1964. One of the principal objectives of the Act is to insure "maximum feasible participation" of the poor in the development and administration of community action programs.[136] Op-

---

132. Report of the Attorney General, *op. cit. supra* note 131, at 31. The Report also notes: "Two court clerks, each of whom had served in separate courts for more than twenty years, advised Justice Investigators that they had never seen a verdict for the defendant in any civil case in their courts." *Id.* at 26.

133. The Report notes:

> Many constables own and operate their own registered collection agencies. Other constables simply advertise themselves as being in the collection business, while a third group of constables function as collection agents without forming a separate agency or openly advertising as such. . . . When money is obtained from a debtor, the constable collects not only a fee for serving process in the case, but also retains from 25 per cent to 50 per cent of the amount collected. . . .
>
> As a result, constables are engaging in practices designed to terrify the average citizen and to make it clear to debtors that by reason of the constable's close association with the magistrate who will hear the case, any attempt to resist collection is futile.

Id. at 27.

134. "One magistrate conceded that his wife was half owner of a collection agency which obtained 25 per cent to 50 per cent of sums recovered. Without apparent concern, the magistrate admitted the fact that he had a personal pecuniary interest in cases where he sat in judgment when he said: '. . . I handle all this business for one reason. If my wife makes money, I'm going to benefit by it because I have an opportunity to spend some of the money she makes, being the president of the company that employs the Constable who handles the work.'" *Id.* at 28.

135. *Id.* at 29.

136. Section 202 of the Economic Opportunity Act of 1964 (Public Law 88-452) states in part: "The term 'community action program' means a program . . . which is developed, conducted and administered with the maximum feasible participation of the groups served." 78 Stat. 516 (1964).

position to this policy, particularly on the part of local political leaders,[137] highlights some of the difficulties of establishing an effective constituency among the poor.

Passivity. The effectiveness of agencies designed to serve the poor is frequently undermined by a tendency to adopt a passive rather than an active stance. These agencies do not ordinarily seek ways to extend the law to the advantage of the poor, and they are less than fully committed to developing new rights and remedies or to educating or encouraging their poor constituents to assert their rights. Rather, they remain inert until moved by the complaint of an interested party with standing. Given an apathetic clientele, this orientation may well defeat their professed aims.

The passive stance is perhaps most evident in agencies charged with the enforcement of legal rights, such as consumer and civil rights commissions. A study of the New Jersey Civil Rights Division notes that although the agency had been given extensive powers, including the authority to initiate enforcement proceedings,

> it narrowly construed its powers to act at all, devised a series of procedural steps which operated against vigorous enforcement, and compromised and settled cases at a rather high rate, with a relatively low level of relief.[138]

Reliance upon the initiation of complaints by the victims of illegal practices has proven to be an ineffective method of law enforcement; most agencies receive

---

137. The San Francisco CHRONICLE, Nov. 5, 1965, p. 22, notes:

The Budget Bureau, fiscal arm of the White House, has told the Office of Economic Opportunity it would prefer less emphasis on involvement of the poor at the policy level in community project planning.

"Maximum feasible participation" of the poor — the language of the law — means, in the Bureau's view, primarily the employment of the poor in carrying out the program, not designing it. . . .

Individuals who read the law differently from the Budget Bureau had heard that the bureau was withholding $35 million to remind the anti-poverty agency that encouraging the poor to organize and raise their voice is unsettling politics.

These individuals believe that pressure for this policy is coming from the big city mayors, most of whom are Democrats.

The mayors have openly protested in the past against demands of the poor for policy planning positions. The mayors see a threat to their patterns for governing cities and to their own political security if the poor develop into militant city hall lobbies.

138. A. Blumrosen, *Antidiscrimination Laws in Action in New Jersey: A Law-Sociology Study*, 19 RUTGERS L. REV., 187, 196 (1965).

only a trickle of complaints. Among the reasons advanced for the paucity of victim complaints to human relations commissions are: (1) ignorance of the "existence and facilities of state commissions," (2) lack of confidence in their ability to "provide effective and prompt remedies for discrimination," and (3) aloofness and remoteness of these commissions from the people they purport to serve.[139]

Similar findings are reported with respect to the enforcement of housing code regulations. These agencies, too, wait upon complaints from tenants before taking action, a procedure that has generally failed to achieve the purpose of code enforcement.

> Complaint-initiated inspections alone are unlikely to result in effective code enforcement for a number of reasons. First, such inspections tend to focus only on the alleged violations. Thus, a deteriorated building may be inspected and repaired on a piecemeal basis. Second, because many violations inevitably go unreported, random enforcement results . . . Third, the uneven enforcement pattern reduces incentives to voluntary compliance.[140]

Agency preference for party initiative is reinforced and perhaps motivated by a commitment to seeking voluntary compliance through conciliation. "The rationale offered by the Massachusetts [human relations] commission [for failing to initiate complaints] is that the initiation of enforcement proceedings is inconsistent with the commission's function of adjusting complaints through conciliation."[141] The agency's task, then, is not to vindicate the rights of aggrieved parties, or to punish those who have violated these rights, but rather to bring about a "satisfactory adjustment." Such a policy tends to undermine the legal principles at stake; it may also be self-defeating. With respect to the enforcement of housing code regulations it has been observed:

> [T]here is some danger that a preoccupation with encouraging voluntary compliance will stall the enforcement process; the compliance period itself probably engenders landlord delay in correcting violations. Philadelphia discontinued its compliance board in 1963 primarily because of overreliance on time extensions, which inordinately delayed resort to court prosecutions . . . A study in Chicago . . . found that 85 per cent of the cases were continued at least once, with an average of two and one-half continuances per case, and that the number of continuances was greater in cases involving a large number of violations.[142]

---

139. J. Witherspoon, *supra* note 82, at 1191.

140. Comment, *Enforcement of Municipal Housing Codes*, 78 HARV. L. REV. 801, 807 (1965).

141. J. Witherspoon, *supra* note 82, at 1192, where he notes: "Although a few state human relations commissions have authority to file complaints initiating enforcement proceedings, they have, by and large, rarely done so."

142. Comment, *supra* note 140, at 815, 819.

The complaint-oriented agency tends to focus on *individual* violations; it does not attempt to alter the structural conditions that lead to widespread violation. A few human relations commissions have adopted a more affirmative posture, calling for "the employment of such techniques as negotiation and education to induce broad sectors of private industry or government to take constructive action in opening up [employment] opportunities for minorities on a broad scale."[143]

It should be noted that the conclusions advanced as to the ineffectiveness of conciliation in altering discriminatory practices or in enforcing housing code regulations, although plausible, are not supported by hard data. We are not aware of any systematic studies of the deterrant effect of such agency practices, nor are we aware of any studies which seek to determine empirically the relative effectiveness of different methods of law enforcement in various social contexts. This is clearly an area calling for investigation.

Inadequate Resources. Most agencies and tribunals that deal with the poor have wholly inadequate resources. They have few tools for implementing their decisions and policies, and because of insufficient funds and personnel they are reluctant to enlarge their functions. Legislative bodies are loathe to allocate additional funds unless pressed to do so, and more often than not they are under pressure to limit such aid. As regards welfare administration, the Moreland Commission Report concludes:

> The principal obstacles to preventing dependency and deterioration and restoring recipients to self-care, self-support, or improved functioning is an almost total absence of professionally trained and qualified social workers, inadequate supervision, insufficient in-service training, high caseloads, low salaries, poor working conditions, inadequate assistance grants, and insufficient medical, psychiatric, vocational, housing, day care, and other specialized auxiliary personnel and services. There are fewer than 100 professionally qualified social workers in all intake and undercare units in this State as compared with almost 2,000 required.[144]

Lack of funds and low salaries frustrate the quest for adequate staffs. Public assistance workers tend to be especially poorly paid.[145] Low salaries and burden-

---

143. J. Witherspoon, *supra* note 82, at 1202-03. The author cites the Philadelphia commission as the most successful example of this more effective approach.

144. Report to the Moreland Commission on Welfare, *op. cit. supra* note 119, at 4. Agencies involved in the enforcement of housing code regulations are also hamstrung by lack of funds. Comment, *supra* note 140, at 804.

145. E. MAY, THE WASTED AMERICANS: COST OF OUR WELFARE DILEMMA 113 (1964).

some caseloads lead inevitably to high turnover in personnel. In 1962 the average rate of resignations of caseworkers across the nation was 26 per cent. In California, New York and Illinois it was over 30 per cent; Maryland, with 46 per cent turnover, had the highest rate.[146]

In public welfare agencies unskilled and untrained personnel are the rule rather than the exception.[147] The Moreland Commission reports: "The latest available figures show that 80.6 per cent of the 5,142 investigators, supervisors and executives in New York State's Public Assistance programs had no academic training to fit them for this work."[148] And regardless of their qualifications high turnover means that few caseworkers "have sufficient continuity to get to know their cases well enough to be of help."[149] Higher level administrative personnel in welfare also come under criticism from the Moreland Commission: "Most county welfare commissioners," the report concludes, "lack sufficient educational qualifications for their jobs."[150]

With respect to the courts indications are that judges in lower-level tribunals are generally less experienced and less adequately trained than their colleagues in upper-level courts. In New York City, for example, lower-court judges are younger, have been on the bench and in their current positions for a shorter period of time, and a larger proportion of them are graduates of lower-quality night law schools.[151] The generally low prestige of inferior tribunals contributes to the lesser competence of judges occupying such positions. According to Handler:

> [T]he juvenile court is considered to be the lowest rung on the judicial ladder. Rarely does the court attract men of maturity and ability. The work is not regarded as desirable or appropriate for higher judgeships. In courts of mixed

---

146. *Id.* at 109. Although these states have generally high public assistance salaries relative to other parts of the country, they are still low relative to salaries of other professionals (or quasi-professionals) in the areas cited. It is this latter disparity which probably contributes to high turnover, insofar as salaries are the issue.

147. There is one caseworker with full professional training for every 23,000 relief recipients. One out of three caseworkers in public welfare did not complete an undergraduate education. Only one out of ten has taken any graduate courses in social work. And only one out of a hundred has completed two-year professional social work training. May, *op. cit. supra* note 145, at 104.

148. Public Welfare in the State of New York, *op. cit. supra* note 121, at 70.

149. Report to the Moreland Commission on Welfare, *op. cit. supra* note 119, at 5.

150. *Id.* at 5.

151. J. CARLIN, LAWYERS' ETHICS 85-86 (1966).

jurisdiction, judges seek to avoid assignment to the juvenile division and rotation must be employed.[152]

In California, which has a consolidated court system, assignment to those departments that generally deal with the poor usually goes to the newest and therefore least experienced man.[153]

Lower court judges are not only less competent than higher court judges, they may also be less committed to the purposes of the court. Thus, many judges in landlord-tenant and housing courts are reported to be "unsympathetic to housing code prosecutions."[154] High turnover, low morale, burdensome paper work and lack of communication with upper levels of the agency weaken the commitment of caseworkers in public assistance programs to department policies.[155]

Deficient remedies. Available remedies tend to be oriented toward the problems and interests of the more affluent users of legal agencies; they are frequently of little value in meeting the needs of the poor. On the one hand the plaintiff's situation may be little changed for the better by a favorable decision. On the other hand, those whose claims and grievances are similar to the plaintiff's may be little served.

The courts' are often helpless before problems repeatedly brought to them by lower class clients. We are familiar with this situation in the criminal process; many judges, for example, have decried the uselessness of putting those repeatedly arrested for public drunkenness through what has been termed the "revolving door" of the local jail. On the civil side it may be asked whether a lower class wife is at all aided by a decision that she has a right to support from her impecunious husband, or whether her situation is improved by confining the husband to jail for violating a support order. One judge expressed his sense of helplessness in this way:

> [In lower-class maintenance cases] you are the umpire in an impossible dispute. You feel the least satisfaction because there is no workable solution. You are not going to give the wife enough money, nor are you going to leave enough money for the husband to get along on. These questions are beyond me.[156]

---

152. J. Handler, *The Juvenile Court and the Adversary System: Problems of Function and Form,* 1965 WIS. L. REV. 10, 17 (1965).

153. Based on our field interviews with several California state court judges.

154. See Comment, *supra* note 140, at 823.

155. See Public Welfare in the State of New York, *op. cit. supra* note 121, at 79.

156. Drawn from our field notes.

It is important to stress that the sense of helplessness expressed by our informant is not unique; it is not the product of a special, individual sensitivity. Instead, it is widespread; and it appears to be a function of a legal process that has often failed to develop adequately to meet the actual situation of litigants.

Perhaps the most serious deficiency of many existing legal remedies is their impotence before such institutionalized violations or evasions of law as deceptive practices on the part of manufacturers and merchants, housing code violations by slum landlords and racial discrimination in employment and housing. In the face of these practices the sanctions available to legal agencies seem puny indeed. Thus, enforcement of housing standards relies heavily upon the use of fines. But fines are generally too light to be effective. If the penalty is light, it can be written off easily by the landlord as part of his operating expenses. Even repeated fines may be less costly than making needed repairs.[157]

Inadequate remedies also impair the effectiveness of civil rights commissions. The principal failing, according to one study, is the fact that most agencies lack the authority to initiate enforcement proceedings.[158]

CONCLUSION

Where human conduct is subject to law, issues of justice are certain to arise. What is the authoritative rule? Has it been violated? Has it been applied fairly? Was proper notice given? Have the parties had sufficient opportunity to develop proofs and arguments? Is the tribunal biased? These are but a few of the many questions that emerge from and during the settlement of controversies at law.

---

157. On the whole, criminal remedies for code violations have proven inadequate. Their basic problem is that a criminal fine is not well suited to ensuring repair and maintenance. . . .

   When present judicial remedies are surveyed, one is impressed by the degree to which the judicial process hinders adequate code enforcement. The courts seem unable to process violations efficiently. . . . Then, too, with the exception of equity proceedings, courts often have difficulty in bringing the necessary parties before them, while agencies, to achieve compliance, prosecute those who can be found rather than those actually responsible.

Comment, *supra* note 140, at 826, 830-31.

158. A major structural defect of most state human relations commissions is that although they may initiate investigations, they have no authority to file complaints for the purpose of instituting enforcement proceedings. Surely no more disabling requirement, or one less consistent with their mission, could have been imposed upon these agencies. . . .

J. Witherspoon, *supra* note 82, at 1191.

We have conventionally seen courts as the site of adjudication. This process, however, may take place elsewhere, most particularly in administrative settings before specially constituted tribunals. We need to study adjudication in its many settings and we need to explore the forms it takes. Studies of courts are insufficient; studies of adjudication in other contexts are similarly inadequate. The immediate task, here as elsewhere in the sociology of law, is to formulate questions that will facilitate empirical inquiry and the development of sociological theory. In this case what is needed is a theory of the adjudicative process.

Study of the legal encounters of poor persons can help to further our understanding of adjudication and the adversary system.[159] Two matters stand out.

First, issues for adjudication involving the poor frequently arise in administrative as well as judicial settings, where cases are commonly processed without the benefit of an adversary system or conventional procedural safeguards. In some tribunals the presence of these arrangements is thought to disrupt the efficient production of routinized decisions; in others there is a virtual abandonment of such procedural devices as being inconsistent with the purposes of the tribunal.

Second, many of the issues brought before tribunals by and in relation to poor persons do not in any simple sense involve questions for adjudication; that is, the facts are not at issue, nor are the rules. What usually is at issue is the question, What shall we do? On the criminal side this is often clearly recognized. It seems equally true on the civil side. What shall we do about and for this person who has

---

159. When our attention is directed to "legal" disputes, we quickly find that the notion of an "adversary system" becomes central. The exact referrant of this term remains somewhat vague, but it clearly refers to something beyond the fact that disputes necessarily involve adversaries. A method of adjudication seems at issue, a method entailing institutionalized procedures intended to produce "sides" committed to the development and presentation of a point of view about the facts and legal questions at hand. "Representatives" who are experts at developing and presenting such points of view are typically included in the idea of an adversary system, as well as a neutral third party, the "adjudicator" who decides. The benefits of such a system are vigorously debated. Some contend that it is the best device known to develop facts, and an important vehicle for drawing out the meaning of the law. Others claim that it clouds issues and distorts facts. It is assumed by some that were they given a free reign officials would restrict adversary presentation in the interests of increasing their own freedom of action and their efficiency in disposing of the mountains of cases that often confront them. Under some circumstances, however, officials appear to welcome and foster adversary proceedings and feel that without them their job cannot easily or properly be done. Finally, it is commonly contended that an adversary proceeding is necessary to restrict official arbitrariness, that it is an essential device for holding officials accountable to rules. Little, however, is surely known; none of these matters has been subject to intensive, systematic inquiry.

not paid his rent, who has not met his installment-contract obligations, who needs support for herself and her children? Declarations of rights and duties may seem of little avail in such circumstances. Nevertheless, individuals continue to require protection against arbitrary decisions, particularly when they are backed by punitive sanctions. How does the legal system provide the needed protection — if it does? What is the fate of adjudication when it is primarily "results" that are sought? Does emphasis on "rehabilitation" or "social therapy" conflict with a concern for legal accountability?

Study of the administration of law affecting the poor also highlights the frequent ineffectiveness of legal agencies in coping with the legal problems of the poor. As we have noted, our institutions for administering law in civil matters are essentially passive; they remain inert until moved by the complaint of an aggrieved party. Absent such initiative — and the poor characteristically do not take initiative — justice generally will not be done. This contrasts sharply with the criminal process, which includes a state apparatus, in many circumstances self-initiating, to prosecute violations of law. What accounts for this difference? What assumptions underly it?

Furthermore, available remedies that depend on the action of private parties in specific controversies are usually inadequate or inappropriate even in the short run; they appear to be incapable of insuring even a minimum of legal protection and control. Such means are perhaps most effective when used to deter or remedy infrequent lapses in a context of generally lawful conduct. When illegality becomes commonplace the worth of these remedies is considerably reduced. What alternatives are there? What are the conditions under which they are likely to arise and be sustained?

A fundamental condition accounting for the indifference of those who operate the legal system to the needs and interests of the poor is the evident inability of the poor to become organized into effective constituents of legal agencies. This leads us to inquire into the political context of legal institutions and those community forces that shape the character and aims of such institutions. Moreover, we are led to ask how a disadvantaged clientele can develop into an effective constituency, and to consider the conditions that prevent this from taking place. This brings us to an examination of the character of legal representation for the poor and their capacity to make effective use of the law.

LEGAL REPRESENTATION AND THE POOR

The more fully developed a legal order, the greater the need for persons capable of formulating and challenging the reasons upon which the authority of claims, decisions or actions is based.[160] The specialized responsibility for carrying out these critical functions may be located in a variety of social roles. In the Anglo-American system of law this responsibility has traditionally been assumed by the legal profession. Study of the role of the legal profession in relation to the poor directs our attention to the wide variation in the character and quality of legal services provided different classes in society.

CHARACTER OF LEGAL SERVICE FOR THE POOR

Existing studies indicate that the poor are least likely to use lawyers, that when they do they generally have access to the least competent and least responsible members of the bar, and that such assistance as they are provided is generally of a quite limited character. Let us consider first the services provided the poor by private attorneys.

Surveys conducted in several states indicate that about two out of three lower class families have *never* employed a lawyer, compared with about one out of three upper class families.[161] A recent study of lawyers in private practice in New York City found that less than five per cent reported the median income of their individual clients to be under $5,000 a year, although half the families and unrelated individuals in New York City had incomes under this amount. Conversely, 70 per cent of the lawyers reported that the median income of their clients was over $10,000, yet less than 10 per cent of New York's families and unrelated individuals received incomes that high.[162]

The relatively few private attorneys available to the poor tend to be the least well trained and the least likely to conform even to the minimal standards of the bar. These lawyers are invariably at the lower end of the profession in quality of training and level of academic achievement,[163] and because of the insecurity of their practice they are most likely to succumb to temptations to exploit clients.[164]

Legal services rendered the poor are apt to be restricted in scope and limited in effectiveness. Cases are not usually accepted unless there is a clear cause of

---

160. See P. Nonet & J. Carlin, *The Legal Profession,* in INT'L ENCYC. SOC. SCI. (in press, p. 4 of the article), for a fuller discussion of this point.

161. J. Carlin & J. Howard, *Legal Representation and Class Justice,* 12 U.C.L.A. L. REV. 381, 382-83 (1965).

162. J. Carlin, *op. cit. supra* note 151, at 178, based on interviews with a random sample of 800 lawyers in private practice in Manhattan and the Bronx.

163. *Id.* at 22-30.

164. *Id.* at 71-73.

action and a fairly certain return — that is, unless the case in effect pays for itself. A personal injury case handled on a contingent fee basis is the prime example.[165] Because fees are usually small, when poor clients are accepted, lawyers are ordinarily reluctant to devote much time or energy to their problems, and there is usually little incentive to go much beyond the case as presented.[166] Legal service is characteristically too little and too late. The poor man usually waits too long before seeking legal help; if he comes to a lawyer at all it is generally after he has been arrested, after his goods have been repossessed or after his wages have been attached. Because the poor are financially insecure, their lawyers are often under considerable pressure to seek quick settlements. There is rarely any interest in raising or pursuing legal principles that would have relevance beyond the case at hand.

To supplement private legal representation special agencies have been created for the express purpose of extending legal services to the indigent. These include assigned counsel and public defender systems in criminal cases and Legal Aid in civil cases. With respect to the representation of criminal defendants, there is considerable evidence to suggest that neither the assigned counsel nor public defender system as now constituted is capable of providing adequate service to the indigent accused. A large proportion of poor defendants (particularly in misdemeanor cases) are not represented at all. Moreover, when counsel is provided he frequently has neither the resources, the skill nor the incentive to defend his client effectively; and he usually enters the case too late to make any real difference in the outcome.[167] Indeed, the generally higher rate of guilty pleas and prison sentences among defendants represented by assigned counsel or the public defender suggest that these attorneys may actually undermine their clients' position.[168]

---

165. Data obtained in a survey of auto accident victims in New York City show that in attempting to recover for losses resulting from their injuries lower-class individuals are as likely as upper-class individuals to hire attorneys. J. Carlin, "How Accident Victims Get to Lawyers," unpublished memorandum, Bureau of Applied Social Research, Columbia University, 1959.

166. See H. O'Gorman, Lawyers and Matrimonial Cases 61 (1963).

167. J. Carlin and J. Howard, *supra* note 161, at 418-21.

168. The Attorney General's Committee on Poverty and the Administration of Criminal Justice concluded:

> In the judgment of the Committee present practices sometimes induce a plea of guilty because appointed counsel recognize the futility of electing to contest in the absence of resources to litigate effectively. The facts indicate that in all the districts studied, pleas of guilty are entered much more frequently by defendants with assigned counsel, than those represented by private counsel. Thus, in the Northern District of Illinois in fiscal 1961, an

Legal Aid organizations have been seriously handicapped in meeting the vast potential need for legal representation among the poor and in dealing with the cases that are actually handled. Resources are grossly inadequate. Less than 4 million dollars was spent in 1963 to finance the operations of all Legal Aid organizations in the United States handling civil cases. This figure represents less than two-tenths of one per cent of the total expenditures for legal services in the United States in 1963.[169] Largely because of its meager resources Legal Aid has just barely managed to keep up with the expanding population. In 1963 it was processing about the same number of new cases per thousand population as in 1916.[170] Lacking sufficient staff and funds, Legal Aid organizations have been understandably reluctant to extend or advertise their services. Rather, there is a marked fear of opening the flood gates, of becoming swamped with new cases. Furthermore, high caseloads[171] frequently lead to a mass processing of cases and thus to routinized,

---

> initial plea of guilty was entered by approximately 75% of all defendants represented by assigned counsel whereas the figure was about 20% in cases represented by private counsel. . . . The Committee has also concluded that the deficiencies of the present (assigned counsel) system adversely affect the quality of the defense made. In the San Francisco Division . . . some 42% of defendants represented by assigned counsel were sentenced to prison while about 29% of those represented by private counsel received prison terms.

POVERTY AND THE ADMINISTRATION OF FEDERAL CRIMINAL JUSTICE 29 (1963). In the Sacramento Division 77% of defendants with assigned counsel were imprisoned compared to 42% of those who retained private counsel. *Id.* at 139. The magnitude of these differences suggest that something more is involved here than the possibility that assigned counsel handle weaker cases than private attorneys.

A recent study of a Public Defender Office in a metropolitan California community discloses that public defenders are primarily concerned with obtaining a guilty plea "wherever possible" in order to avoid trial. The underlying assumption is that those who are charged with crimes are guilty:

> The P.D.'s activity is seldom geared to securing acquittals for clients. He and the D.A., as co-workers in the same courts, take it for granted that the persons who come before the courts are guilty of crimes and are to be treated accordingly. . . . As we shall argue below, the way defendants are "represented," (the station manning rather than assignment of counsellors to clients), the way trials are conducted, the way interviews are held and the penal code employed — all of the P.D.'s work is premised on the supposition that people charged with crimes have committed crimes.

D. Sudnow, *Normal Crimes: Sociological Features of the Penal Code in Public Defender Office,* 12 SOCIAL PROBLEMS 269 (1965).

169. J. Carlin & J. Howard, *supra* note 161, at 410.

170. *Id.* at 408-09 n.110.

171. For example, the caseload in the Los Angeles office approximated 2,000 cases per attorney per year. *Id.* at 416.

perfunctory service. Three out of four accepted applicants for legal aid receive only a single brief consultation; only a minimal amount of time is given to the investigation of facts, to legal research and drafting of legal documents and to court work.[172] Many offices, in fact, are incapable of handling cases that require extensive investigation or time-consuming litigation. The situation is further aggravated by low salaries, high turnover in personnel and inadequate direction "by disinterested or inactive boards of directors."[173] There is little time or incentive to enter into a contest over legal principles, to make or alter law or to combat institutionalized sources of injustice.

The effectiveness of Legal Aid is also limited by its vulnerability to pressure from local bar and business interests which are its principal financial supporters. The local bar insists upon a strict application of financial eligibility requirements to insure that all cases are excluded that might possibly yield a fee to a private attorney. As a result, close to a fifth of all applicants to Legal Aid are annually rejected on financial grounds.[174] Pressure from local businessmen has led to the exclusion of bankruptcy cases in many Legal Aid offices,[175] and it has resulted in a reluctance to press claims against local merchants, landlords and others whose interests would be threatened by more vigorous representation.[176] The tendency, therefore, is for Legal Aid to become a captive of its principal financial supporters

---

172. *Id.* at 416-17.

173. *Id.* at 410.

174. *Id.* at 411.

175. Brownell claims that "the chief reason for the brankruptcy rule seems to be the desire not to lose the good will of merchants and other creditors from whom the societies must seek settlements for their clients." Others have perhaps been more candid by indicating that what is feared is not simply loss of good will but the loss of Legal Aid funds. Several participants at the 1948 conference of NALAO observed: "that they encountered objection to their handling (of) these (bankruptcy) cases from merchants, doctors, small loan companies and others who contribute generously to the Community Chest."

Id. at 415. In 1963 local Community Chests provided 53% of the funds for Legal Aid societies. 1963 ANNUAL REPORT OF NATIONAL LEGAL AID AND DEFENDER ASSOCIATION.

176. Similar pressure may affect the new federally financed legal service programs. Note the following comment of an opponent of a proposed legal service program to be funded by the Office of Economic Opportunity:

Pittsburgh Attorney Alan Williams told the county board of supervisors that landlords, merchants and taxpayers would be among the big losers if the county accepted the proposal put forward by the Contra Costa County Bar Assn. . . . Attorney Williams told the supervisors that the landlords and

who may well be considered its real clients. This leads to a cautious, passive and accommodative posture on the part of Legal Aid attorneys.

It is also important to note that Legal Aid attorneys often conceive of legal service to the poor as a charity or privilege rather than a right. This paternalistic orientation is most evident in the handling of divorce cases. The general view is that divorce is a luxury that should be granted only if the client is deemed morally deserving or if it is absolutely necessary "to protect either the wife or the children from immediate or threatened physical harm, or moral jeopardy."[177] Otherwise, it is felt separation would be an acceptable alternative.[178]

This view of the poor client as incapable of knowing his own best interests — as an irresponsible and immature person — not only undermines the dignity and self respect of the client but it also weakens the capacity of Legal Aid attorneys to recognize legal rights and to seek effective legal solutions. For the poor client, Legal Aid often becomes another line to wait in, another humiliating experience and a further reminder that the law is unresponsive to, if not opposed to, his interests. The experience of the poor with Legal Aid and the effect of this experience on their attitudes toward and willingness to use the law deserve serious study.

FUNCTIONS OF LEGAL REPRESENTATION

What are the functions lawyers might perform that would result in more effective representation of the poor?[179] The following catalogue of functions reflects the need to move beyond the kinds of service the poor have so far been receiving

---

merchants would pay because free counsel for the debtors could avoid payments for months and in the case of landlords could keep tenants in their units for more months with free rent.

Opposition was also based on the contention that the program "will result in the poor bringing suit in civil matters over trivial things." Berkeley DAILY GAZETTE, January 12, 1966, p. 13.

    177. J. Carlin & J. Howard, *supra* note 161, at 415.

    178. Thus, according to the attorney in charge of Legal Aid in Pittsburgh, Pa.:

People may say that poverty prevents (the poor) from having the same rights to get a divorce as a person with money, yet we must remember obtaining a divorce is not a right but a privilege. For most Legal Aid clients, a separation is just as useful and practical as a divorce.

Id. at 413.

    179. In formulating the functions of legal representation, we are indebted to E. Cahn & J. Cahn, *The War on Poverty: A Civilian Perspective*, 73 YALE L.J. 1317 (1964). This essay offers an illuminating statement of the lawyer's role in extending the rule of law to the poor.

to a much closer approximation of the wider range of services enjoyed by the more advantaged segments of the society.

Asserting legal rights which, although recognized in law, remain unimplemented.

Claims and defenses available to the poor often remain unasserted because of the absence of counsel. State housing codes which require landlords to provide heat, water and electricity and to keep the premises free of vermin are frequently violated by slum landlords. Without counsel poor tenants cannot realistically be expected to force compliance. Fraud and misrepresentation in the sale of consumer goods and illegal collection practices could be challenged on the basis of established legal doctrine, but without the assistance of counsel the poor consumer is virtually without recourse; indeed, his very inactivity as well as the inappropriateness of his actions may lead him into further trouble:

> The slum dweller who buys unwisely can hardly be expected to know his liabilities or his rights of recourse against his seller, even if firmly established under law. He does not understand that he must pay for goods even though repossessed, that unrelated possessions can be attached for nonpayment of the purchased goods, or that additions for court costs, marshals' fees, and interest can multiply the original debt.

> Often he mistakenly believes his legal remedy against a fraudulent seller is to stop paying.[180]

In the area of public welfare those who might be eligible for assistance are often improperly denied aid, and benefits may be illegally delayed or terminated. Moreover, some authors believe that methods for determining fraud sometimes lead to unconstitutional invasions of the right to privacy. It is unlikely that such abuses will be remedied so long as the poor lack competent legal representation.

Facilitating the development of legal rights in areas where the law is now vague or biased.

The poor live in a legal universe which has, by and large, been ignored by legal scholars. Low visibility decisions decide their destiny; official discretion

---

180. P. WALD, LAW AND POVERTY 1965 27-28 (1965). David Caplovitz notes:
> When dissatisfied with shoddy merchandise they receive, some families retaliate for the merchant's bad faith by withholding payments. But this logic, which may well make sense in a traditional society and even in dealings with ethical merchants in our bureaucratic society, does not apply in the low-income marketing system. As most of these families soon learned, the contracts they signed precluded this form of redress.

D. CAPLOVITZ, THE POOR PAY MORE 157 (1963).

determines their fate; and rights, even with lawyers to assert them, take a destructively long time to ascertain and vindicate.[181]

Lawyers are obviously needed to develop rights that are now only weakly recognized, to help clarify and fashion the law to allow the poor a greater measure of the protections and benefits that the law could be made to provide. Furthermore, as we have seen, much law tends to be biased against the poor, and competent representation might not only serve to "delay or nullify its operation" but may also "prompt reassessment and change."[182] Accomplishment of these tasks requires skilled advocates to present the interests and claims of the poor before a myriad of decision makers. This would include careful preparation of legal arguments before appellate tribunals and effective lobbying in administrative and legislative bodies.

Bringing pressure to bear to increase the fairness and reasonableness of adjudicative procedures and to insure more positive and sympathetic implementation of legal policies.

One of the basic contributions lawyers can make to the administration of justice is to insist upon adequate procedures for safeguarding the right of parties to a fair hearing and reasoned judgment. As noted in the Report of the Joint Conference on Professional Responsibility:

> In a very real sense it may be said that the integrity of the adjudicative process itself depends upon the participation of the advocate . . . The institution of advocacy is not a concession to the frailties of human nature, but an expression of human insight in the design of a social framework within which man's capacity for impartial judgment can attain its fullest realization.[183]

Because the poor rarely have the assistance of a skilled advocate they have little protection against the frequently capricious exercise of official discretion. Competent advocates for the poor would help remedy this situation. They could also increase the responsiveness of agencies to the special needs and interests of the poor and encourage more active and effective implementation of the law on their behalf.

Assisting in the creation of contractual relations and legal associations to maximize the opportunities and benefits the law provides.

---

181. E. Cahn & J. Cahn, *supra* note 179, at 1340.

182. *Id.* at 1341.

183. *Report of the A.B.A. Joint Conference on Professional Responsibility,* 44 A.B.A.J. 1159, 1160-61 (1958).

It is this activity more than any other which permits the marshalling of the resources of the law for the realization of common interests and aspirations.

> In our society the great bulk of human relations are set, not by governmental decree, but by the voluntary action of the affected parties. Men come together to collaborate and to arrange their relations in many ways; by forming corporations, partnerships, labor unions, clubs and churches; by concluding contracts and leases; by entering a hundred other large and small transactions by which their rights and duties toward one another are defined.
>
> Successful voluntary collaboration usually requires for its guidance something equivalent to a formal charter, defining the terms of the collaboration, anticipating and forfending against possible disputes, and generally providing a framework for the parties' future dealings. In our society the natural architect of this framework is the lawyer.[184]

Lawyers serving well-to-do individuals or large business clients devote the major portion of their energies to the performance of these tasks. In representing poor clients, however, lawyers rarely if ever assist in establishing contractual relations or other forms of legal association. Nevertheless, this kind of representation could be of vital significance to the poor by helping to provide them with an organizational base for more effective participation in and use of the legal order. As will be noted below, legal competence is related to and also supported by political or civic competence. Similarly, legal representation may be seen as political as well as legal in nature. Lawyers not only help to assert and establish claims of right, they also provide a voice for their clients in the decision-making process; and the latter is often an essential precondition for the former. It has been observed that, "the power to create legal relationships is a form of political power."[185] By helping to organize the poor the lawyer in effect serves to enlarge their political competence, and this in turn may further enhance their capacity for more effective use of the law.

CONDITIONS LEADING TO INADEQUATE REPRESENTATION

The functions of the lawyer outlined above are only rarely performed for the poor either by private attorneys or by lawyers specially charged with serving the indigent. What are the conditions that prevent the legal profession from extending and enlarging its services to the poor? The answer lies partly in the fact that the poor lack the competence and resources that would allow them to obtain more adequate representation. We must also consider, however, certain structural characteristics of the legal profession and the traditional orientation of lawyers to clients and their problems.

---

184. *Id.* at 1161.
185. E. Cahn & J. Cahn, *supra* note 179, at 1339.

Structure of rewards

Success in the legal profession as in other occupations is largely measured by the size of one's income. Since the financing of legal services still rests primarily on the principle of fee for service, the poor man is generally an undesirable client. The size of the anticipated fee is not only a factor in the decision to represent a client,[186] it also affects the quality of service provided — for example, decisions about type of action, place of jurisdiction and preparation of the case.[187]

Prestige in the legal profession is also a function of the class and ethnic background of the lawyer's clientele and certain characteristics of the clients' legal problems. High status clients who provide a continuous supply of legal business involving challenging legal problems are considered the most valued clients. In these respects the poor have little to offer. Among the salient features of a lower class clientele are: (1) the presence of clients from ethnic and racial minorities;[188] (2) lack of resources leading to little incentive to treat their problems as other than "cut and dried" legal cases; (3) the non-recurring character of the legal problems ordinarily brought to the lawyer (like personal injury, divorce, crime) leading to a highly unstable and insecure practice,[189] and (4) the necessity of contact with those levels of the administration of justice that are least likely to welcome vigorous presentation of the client's case and most likely to require compromise of ethical

---

186. A study of individual practitioners in Chicago, for example, showed that most lawyers had turned away clients, mainly for economic reasons. Based on further analysis of interview data from the study reported in J. CARLIN, LAWYERS ON THEIR OWN (1962).

187. See H. O'Gorman, *op. cit. supra* note 166, at 61.

188. Among lawyers in private practice in New York City, the less affluent their clientele the more likely they are to represent at least some Negro clients: 58 per cent of those with the least affluent clientele, compared to 1 per cent of those with the most affluent clientele, report that 4 per cent or more of their clients are Negroes. See J. Carlin, *op. cit. supra* note 151.

189. Pertinent findings from the study of New York City lawyers are presented in the table, below:

Index of Client Status	% of Lawyers Handling Mainly Personal Injury, Divorce, Crime	% Having an Unstable (High Turnover) Clientele	% Reporting Great Deal of Competition from Other Lawyers, and That They Have Been Hurt By It
Low	51 (188) }	59	43
Low-Middle	42 (136)		
High-Middle	15 (247) }	28	24
High	0 (194)		

Id. at ch. IV. Number in parentheses refers to the number of respondents.

standards.[190] As a result lawyers generally make every effort to move beyond this kind of practice and bitterly resent their inability to do so. In short, for most lawyers a lower class clientele is a mark of failure.

Party initiative

The reluctance of lawyers to serve the poor also stems from the commitment of the legal system to party initiative, which requires the lawyer to wait upon the presentation of a case or claim before taking action. This does not mean that lawyers must adopt an entirely passive posture. They reformulate issues and facts, recommend certain courses of action and discourage others. It does mean, however, that the client has the responsibility for bringing his case to the attention of the lawyer. The Canons of Ethics deem it unprofessional for a lawyer to solicit "employment by circulars, advertisements, through touters or by personal communications or interviews not warranted by personal relations,"[191] and they forbid lawyers from stirring up litigation by "seeking out those with claims for personal injuries or those having any other grounds of action in order to secure them as clients, or to employ agents or runners for like purposes."[192] A basic assumption of these canons is that parties are competent to initiate claims. But this is not ordinarily true of the poor.

We may well ask why lawyers should not "stir up litigation." The police and prosecuting attorneys do this for the criminal courts; what would happen were lawyers to do so on the civil side? Should solicitation be prohibited if lawyers are thereby able to inform persons of their legally protected rights? What of moving a community to protest en masse some common legal grievance: is this the proper work of attorneys? What is it that is thought to be lost if a more active orientation were adopted? Are these beliefs well grounded?

Focus on the particular case or controversy

Lawyers tend to restrict their attention to the case at hand and to the particular parties to the controversy or action. This reflects in part the preference of the common law tradition for counseling in specific controversies between defined

---

190. Among lawyers in New York City, 41 per cent of those representing the lowest status clients come into contact primarily with the lowest level courts and agencies, compared to 4 per cent of those representing the highest status clients. Further, the lower the level of court and agency contact, the more likely lawyers are to violate the ethical standards of the bar. *Ibid.*

191. Canon 27 of the Canons of Professional Ethics of the American Bar Association. See H. Drinker, Legal Ethics 316-17 (1954).

interests on a case by case basis. And the case-method of instruction still employed by most American law schools undoubtedly reinforces this traditional orientation. The legal problems 'of the poor, however, characteristically arise from systematic abuses embedded in the operation of various public and private agencies, affecting large numbers of similarly situated individuals. Effective solution of these problems may require the lawyer to direct his attention away from a particular claim or grievance to the broader interests and policies at stake, and away from the individual client to a class of clients, in order to challenge more directly and with greater impact certain structural sources of injustice. Consequently, if the lawyer conceives of the poor man's problems as basically separate and individual he may achieve at best only a temporary and limited accommodation of a particular grievance without altering established policies and institutionalized practices. Thus, an attorney representing a welfare recipient may consider it unwise for his client to appeal a decision on eligibility so long as a satisfactory informal adjustment is offered by the welfare agency. He may, however, be turning down an important opportunity to challenge and possibly alter a particularly harsh regulation or rule adversely affecting many other welfare recipients.

It may be necessary, therefore, to supplement or replace individual representation with other forms of advocacy that would serve to aggregate the demands of the poor and allow for more planned presentation of claims to give the poor a more meaningful voice in the legal process and greater leverage in the promotion and protection of their ·interests. These other forms of representation might include: *organizational advocacy* — legal services provided to an organization representing the common or collective interests of a group, or made available to members of the group through its intervention; and *strategic advocacy* — issues selected and generated for the purpose of challenging established practices and for pressing recognition of new rights.[193]

Although rarely employed on behalf of the poor, these forms of advocacy are by no means new. Labor unions, trade associations and corporations have for some years secured the services of lawyers to represent and support the legal interests of their members. The newly acquired legitimacy of group legal practice as a result of recent Supreme Court decisions will undoubtedly increase the use

---

192. Canon 28. *Id.* at 319.

193. P. Nonet & J. Carlin, *op. cit. supra* note 160, at 23, 24.

of such arrangements.[194] Moreover, the test case (a form of strategic advocacy) is a widely recognized and not infrequently employed device for developing new law. What changes in the organization of the legal profession would be necessary to bring these forms of legal representation to the poor? What problems would lawyers face in carrying out these tasks? For example, how can the collective interests of the group be championed effectively without sacrificing possibly conflicting interests of particular members?

Conceptions of legal relevance

A lawyer is trained to view persons and events in the light of certain standards of legal relevance. In order to perform his job well the lawyer must be able to translate facts, issues, and problems into legal facts, legal issues and legal problems. This task is made easier when the client speaks the same language as the lawyer and when the matters brought by clients fall into clearly established categories, or are at least presented in ways that are readily translatable. The poor ordinarily do not speak the same language as lawyers, and their problems are least likely to fit into convenient legal categories. Problems with welfare, landlords or local merchants often do not appear to the lawyer as constituting a clear cause of action for the poor client. The attorney's legal training has prepared him to deal with creditor's rights, not debtor's rights; to represent clients before federal regulatory agencies, not before a local welfare agency or police department; to handle stock options and executive pension funds, not unemployment insurance benefits.

It follows, therefore, that although lawyers may readily acknowledge that the poor have problems, they may be reluctant to define them as legal problems. Indeed, there is a tendency to conceive of their problems as basically social or psychological, calling for therapy rather than justice. Moreover, even when a legal problem is detected the attention of the lawyer may shift to some other, more "fundamental," yet non-legal level of concern.[195] The tendency to conceive of the

---

194. See especially Brotherhood of Railroad Trainmen v. Virginia, 377 U.S. 1 (1964); NAACP v. Button, 371 U.S. 415 (1963). See also REPORT OF THE CALIFORNIA STATE BAR'S STANDING COMMITTEE ON GROUP LEGAL SERVICES (1964); Symposium, *The Availability of Counsel and Group Legal Services,* 12 U.C.L.A. L. REV. 279 (1965).

195. The translation of a legal problem into a social or psychological one is more readily achieved in the civil than the criminal area; when life or liberty is not at stake it is easier to avoid legal issues. This undoubtedly contributes to the fact that lawyers are more reluctant in civil than in criminal cases to accept the notion that legal representation is a matter of right. Thus, efforts to extend legal representation to the poor in criminal cases have generally preceded similar efforts in the civil area and have encountered less resistance.

problems of the poor as essentially non-legal is evident among Legal Aid lawyers. The adoption of this perspective weakens the lawyer's capacity to recognize legal rights and seek legal remedies; it also provides him with a seemingly legitimate rationale for perfunctory service and for his reluctance to serve the poor as a lawyer.

FEDERAL INTERVENTION: OEO'S LEGAL SERVICE PROGRAM

With passage of the Economic Opportunity Act of 1964[196] the federal government has assumed responsibility for financing legal services for the poor and for setting policy standards to guide the organization and provision of such services. The orientation of the OEO legal service program represents a major break with the philosophy of traditional legal aid. This is indicated by: (1) the importance placed upon the establishment of neighborhood law offices to increase the accessibility of legal services to the poor; (2) the requirement that the poor be represented on the governing board of the legal service agency to enhance responsiveness to client needs; (3) the adoption of a more aggressive stance in promoting the collective as well as individual interests of the poor, including the use of legal advocacy as an instrument of social change; and (4) concern for insuring the independence of the legal service organization from those vested interests that might be threatened by more vigorous representation of the poor.[197]

Evaluation of the federal program provides a unique opportunity to explore more fully many of the issues that have been raised in this section of the paper. In particular, we are led to inquire into the various dimensions of effective legal service and the social arrangements that would implement effectiveness. What conditions, for example, are likely to support or undermine the independence of the legal service agency? It will be important to consider in this regard the organizational history of the agency, the political struggles and compromises in establishing the agency and the resulting structure of control.

Furthermore, what are the conditions that are likely to promote a more vigorous style of representation? To what extent will this commitment be eroded by the inevitable pressures of practice and ever-increasing caseloads?[198] To what extent will involvement in a multi-service center increase the risk of reducing potential legal

---

196. 78 STAT. 516 (1964), U.S.C. (1964).

197. SEE GUIDELINES FOR LEGAL SERVICE PROGRAMS (Community Action Program, Office of Economic Opportunity, Washington, D.C.). See also E. Cahn & J. Cahn, *supra* note 179.

198. The experience of neighborhood offices funded by OEO suggests that in spite of an increase in number of attorneys, the case load has not decreased.

problems to social welfare problems?[199] To what extent will pressures from vested interests lead to the adoption of a more cautious and accommodative posture?

A factor that will undoubtedly be of major importance in the development of the program is the attitude of the bar. As in the case of Legal Aid there appear to be a number of lawyers who fear a loss of business as a result of extending free legal services.

A more important and pervasive fear is that the bar, especially the organized bar, will lose control over the provision of legal services to the poor. The OEO requirement of "maximum feasible participation" of the poor has been interpreted to mean that the governing boards of these programs should include at least some representatives of the poor. A number of lawyers, including many officials of Legal Aid, bitterly resent this demand.[200] At the National Conference on Law and Poverty in June of 1965 the president of the National Legal Aid and Defender Association indicated that many legal aid societies would withdraw from the OEO program if they are required to reorganize their board of directors to admit "members of the poor and representatives of the poor."[201]

To what extent, then, will the bar itself interfere with the development of the program, or reduce it to a mere extension of the conventional type of Legal Aid service? A more fundamental question, perhaps, is whether it is possible to establish a government-supported legal service program dedicated to stimulating social change, particularly when the changes that are being sought will affect the structure and operation of agencies of government itself?

Important questions are also raised as to the character of the legal service agency. Does the traditional type of private law office (particularly the small, neighborhood office) provide a useful model for agencies serving the poor? It may

---

199. In most areas the legal service agency is located within a center which houses other OEO-supported community action programs providing various welfare services.

200. An attorney in one California county warned his colleagues:

> I ask you to do some soul searching. Do you really want this monster with eight non-lawyers on the board so that we can qualify for a federal handout? . . . It should be done by lawyers — let's have it run on a legal basis, not with laymen telling us what we should do. . . . It should be run and controlled by attorneys.

Drawn from our field notes.

201. T. Voorhees, *Legal Aid—Current Needs and New Directions*, paper delivered at the National Conference on Law and Poverty, Washington, D.C., June 24, 1965.

be necessary to explore and experiment with different forms of organization, different methods of allocating work, new types of specialization. The establishment of a centralized research and planning staff may well be called for to implement the broader, strategic goals of the program. Further, what organizational tools can be devised for processing a large volume of cases? How much of the work of the agency can be routinized without imperilling the effectiveness of the services provided? What functions might be delegated to law students, or perhaps to sub-professionals?

POVERTY AND LEGAL COMPETENCE

Throughout this essay we have said that the poor enjoy fewer of the benefits and protections of the law than the rich. We have attempted to identify some of the conditions of this phenomenon, focusing principally on certain characteristics of the legal system and those who operate the system. We must also take into account the readiness and ability of poor persons to use the law. What qualities are required, and under what social conditions are they likely to emerge?

One view of the citizen's role in the legal system stresses his capacity to evoke favorable consideration from officials in the application of established rules.[202] We would suggest another image of the competence required to use the legal system,

---

202. Such an image is implicit in G. ALMOND & S. VERBA, THE CIVIC CULTURE (1965). The authors characterize administrative or subject competence (as distinguished from political competence) as follows:

> The subject does not participate in making rules, nor does his participation involve the use of political influence. His participation comes at the point at which general policy has been made and is being applied. The competence of the subject is more a matter of being aware of his rights under the rules than of participating in the making of the rules. And though the subject may attempt to make the government official responsive, he appeals rather than demands. His appeal may be to the set of administrative rules that are supposed to guide the action of the government official, or he may appeal to his considerateness. If the government official responds, it is because he is following these rules or because he is being considerate — not because influence has been applied to him. . . . The (competent) subject . . . may want and expect beneficial outputs from government. But he does not expect them to be accorded to him because he demands them. The government official who acts to benefit him responds, not to the subject's demands, but to some other force. . . . This kind of . . . competence is more circumscribed, more passive than that of the citizen. It may set in motion an action that will affect the way in which a rule is interpreted or enforced against an individual. It is not a creative act of influence that can affect the content of the decisions themselves, except in an indirect way.

Id. at 168-69. See *Id.* at 138.

one that emphasizes the ability to further and protect one's interests *through active assertion of legal rights*. We call the relevant ability "legal competence." The legally competent person will want and expect government officials to take his interests into account in both their dealings with him and with others; but he will see their propensity to do so as closely connected with his own actions. The competent subject will take initiative. Moreover, like other practical men, he is concerned with creating, preserving and expanding his capacity to initiate action. He may expect government officials (and others) to accord him "equal treatment" and "serious consideration,"[203] but he will continuously lay a basis for this expectation through his own actions.

As we see him, the competent subject will see law as a *resource* for developing, furthering and protecting his interests. This is partly a matter of knowledge. The competent subject will be aware of the relation between the realization of his interests and the machinery of law making and administration. He will know how to use this machinery and when to use it. Moreover, he will see assertion of his interests through legal channels as desirable and appropriate. This is not to say that he will view law as omni-relevant, as a sort of all-purpose tool. He will be aware of the limits of law. But it is important to stress that he will not be hostile to extension of the rule of law. When he believes it proper, he will make an effort to bring his interests under the aegis of authoritative rules. This will call for "a creative act of influence" that will affect the content of official decisions.

It is implicit in what we have said that the competent subject will have a sense of himself as a *possessor of rights*, and in seeking to validate and implement these rights through law he will be concerned with holding *authorities accountable to law*. With respect to the latter, Almond and Verba contend that in seeking favorable rulings from legal and other government authorities the subject may appeal to "the set of administrative rules that are supposed to guide the action of the government official, or he may appeal to his considerateness."[204] We suggest that the legally competent subject does more than appeal to the considerateness of officials; he *insists* that official actions and decisions be consistent with authoritative rules.

In doing so he changes or reinforces his relationship to those who make and administer law. He changes it in a direction compatible with the rule of law, for

---

203. Almond and Verba asked their respondents whether they expected government officials and the police to accord them "equal treatment" and "serious consideration." If they did expect it, respondents were classified as having a "sense of administrative competence," *i.e.*, as competent "subjects." *Id.* at 70, 72, 168.

204. *Id.* at 168.

his manner of winning "consideration" tends to reduce his dependence on the good will and whims of those who govern.[205] The competent subject demands that there be *reasons* for official decisions and actions, and that these reasons be consonant with both "reason" and "law." Power, however benevolent, is not for him its own justification.

In sum, it is evident that "legal competence" is a complex quality. Broadly speaking it would appear to consist of one part *awareness* and one part *assertiveness*. The legally competent person has a sense of himself as a possessor of rights, and he sees the legal system as a resource for validation of these rights. He knows when and how to seek validation. Beyond this, the legally competent person takes action: he not only "knows his rights" and how to validate them, he turns to the legal system and uses it when his interests can be served by doing so. In the process, he tends to extend the rule of law.

THE FAILURE TO TAKE ACTION

As we have just noted, an essential ingredient of legal competence is a propensity to take action. This requirement is especially critical in the American legal system since a major assumption built into the operating philosophy and structure of our legal institutions, particularly those concerned with civil matters, is that aggrieved parties will take legal initiative. This assumption may hold for the rich under most circumstances; there is considerable reason to believe that it does not hold for the poor. Such data as exist suggest that the poor suffer many legal wrongs but that they rarely attempt to redress their grievances through law.

A study of automobile accident victims in New York City shows a strong relation between low socio-economic status and "doing nothing" about a conventional legal problem. As indicated in the table below, the lower the socio-economic status of respondents the less likely they were to take some action to recover for their losses — that is, to file a claim themselves with an insurance company, or to seek help from a lawyer.[206]

---

205. In discussing administrative competence Almond and Verba suggest that even if subjects "exert pressure on bureaucrats to follow the administrative rules" (versus seeking "a particular decision in favor of a particular individual or group"), "*it does not change the relationship of the individual to the administration* — he still comes as a subject, albeit a competent one, whose appeal is to the rules of the bureaucracy." See *Id.* at 171-72. Emphasis added. We would argue that the competent subject does change this relationship.

206. See J. Carlin, "How Accident Victims Get to Lawyers: Summary of Findings," unpublished manuscript, Bureau of Applied Social Research, Columbia University, 1954.

Socio-Economic Status	Per Cent of Accident Victims Who Made Some Effort to Recover	Number of Respondents
Low (low on income, occupation, and education)*	73	(30)
Lower-Middle (low on two)	84	(45)
Upper-Middle (low on one)	90	(39)
High (low on none)	98	(41)

*Low income is defined as earning $5,000 a year or less; low occupation is defined as laborer; low education is defined as having completed fewer than 4 years of high school.

David Caplovitz has shown that inaction is the most prevalent response among low-income families confronted with consumer problems, problems for which the legal system might provide solutions:

> The families who reported that they had been cheated [more than 40 per cent of the 464 respondents] were asked what they did about their problem. *Half of them did nothing at all;* they did not even complain to the merchant [and those who did nothing were apt to blame themselves for being taken in]. Another 40 per cent tried to deal with the merchant themselves. *Only 9 per cent sought professional help* . . . The apathetic response was by no means limited to cases of overcharging. Some families who were deceived about the price of their appliances, who were victims of substitutions, who were sold defective merchandise, or who were sued by merchants, also did nothing about their problems . . . This sense of resignation was forcefully expressed by a 28 year-old Puerto Rican head of a household who had been on Welfare for eight years. He described an incident in which he had been badly cheated, and when asked what he had done about it, he replied: *"No, we didn't do anything because we can't say anything. We poor against a powerful rich."* [The interviewer noted that this was said humbly, not aggressively.][207]

Leonard Zeitz' study[208] of what Negroes do about discrimination also suggests that the poor tend to be apathetic. Of those respondents asserting that they had personally experienced discrimination (69 of 130 respondents), 87 per cent did

---

Based on interviews conducted in 1957 with 155 persons selected at random from a list of persons reported to the New York State Motor Vehicle Bureau as "mildly" injured in automobile accidents in New York City. See R. Hunting & G. Neuwirth, Who Sues in New York City (1962), for a report of this study.

207. D. Caplovitz, *op. cit. supra* note 180, at 171-72.

208. L. Zeitz, *Survey of Negro Attitudes Toward Law*, 19 Rutgers L. Rev. 288 (1965).

nothing about it. Another 9 per cent failed to say what they did, if anything.[209] Questions intended to probe for the attitudes associated with inaction brought the following kinds of responses:

"You can't do nothing. Just hope men will change." "Mister, I don't go where I'm not wanted." "You can't prove nothing, so why try." "I just don't want no trouble."

Zeitz has this to say about these responses:

They typify the prevailing attitudes. Some, perhaps fearing the dominant whites, "want no trouble"; others feel that their situation is hopeless and will not try; still others belligerently remain in their ghettos, refusing to acknowledge the existence of their problems; and finally some hope, perhaps through prayer, that "men will change." That there is a perception of discrimination is all too clear in our sample, but what is equally clear is the profound inertia gripping the respondents. Their attitude towards legal remedies for ending discrimination is consistent with their attitudes towards their low educational attainment, poor vocational skills, and substandard residences: a recognition of the problem, but *an all-pervasive inertia in doing something about it*.[210]

Data from the "Newsweek poll"[211] suggest that wealthier Negroes are less likely to be gripped by inertia than poor Negroes. The findings show that a larger proportion of middle- and upper-income Negroes than those with lower incomes have participated in direct action protest. The following table summarizes these data.[212]

---

209. *Id.* at 295. Unfortunately for our purpose, Zeitz does not show the class division of those who did and did not take action. Forty-eight per cent of the sample had incomes of less than $5,000; 42 per cent had incomes between $5,000 and $10,000; three per cent had incomes of $10,000 or more. However, Zeitz did analyze the characteristics of Negroes who had brought cases of discrimination to the attention of the New Jersey State Division on Civil Rights from July 1, 1962 through June 30, 1963. These persons were compared with respondents. Division users were significantly better educated and had greater incomes. Twenty per cent of Division users had incomes of less than $5,000, 51 per cent between $5,000 and $10,000, and 29 per cent $10,000 or more.

210. *Id.* at 295. (Emphasis added).

211. W. BRINK & L. HARRIS, THE NEGRO REVOLUTION IN AMERICA (1964).

212. *Id.* at 203, table "Question 24a, Negro Participation in Direct Action." It is worth noting, however, that class differences were considerably reduced when the question was whether the respondent would be willing to participate. This suggests that some part of the explanation of inaction — at least in demonstrations, picketing, etc. — may be that poor persons are not as privy as others to opportunities to participate. See *Id.* at 203, table "Question 24b, Negro Willingness to Participate in Direct Action."

NEGRO PARTICIPATION IN DIRECT ACTION

	NON-SOUTH			SOUTH	
	Total Non-South %	Low Income %	Lower Middle Income %	Middle and Upper Income %	Total South %	Middle and Upper Income %
Stopped buying at a store.	28	6	25	63	38	79
Marched in a demonstration.	14	13	10	44	11	30
Picketed a store.	9	6	7	23	10	30
Taken part in a sit-in.	7	13	6	12	9	28
Gone to jail.	3	—	3	2	6	15

In the balance of this section we shall suggest how some of the features of the life-situation of the poor contribute to their inability to make effective use of the law. Our characterization of the situation of poverty draws heavily on a recent paper by Albert K. Cohen and Harold M. Hodges, Jr. depicting the "Characteristics of the Lower Blue-Collar Class."[213] We shall discuss briefly four aspects of the situation of poverty: (1) the "narrow world" of the poor; (2) powerlessness; (3) failure to develop and participate in issue-oriented organizations; and (4) the experience of the poor with the legal system itself.

NARROW WORLD

Those who have studied the poor portray them as living in a comparatively "narrow world": a world of "solidary familiars." Within this sheltered environment, Cohen and Hodges note, the poor person "can move with some confidence, some security, some sense of trust, and with dignity. Outside of this world he feels weak, uncertain, disparaged, and distrustful."[214] Caplovitz paints a similar picture. The poor consumer, he says, is steeped in "traditionalism," fearful of leaving his own circumscribed sector of the city, "intimidated by the impersonality that pervades the major downtown stores."[215] This partially self-imposed confinement may limit

---

213. A. Cohen & H. Hodges, Jr., *Characteristics of the Lower Blue-Collar Class*, 10 SOCIAL PROBLEMS 303 (1963).

214. *Id.* at 308.

215. D. Caplovitz, *op. cit. supra* note 180, at 181.

the capacity of the poor to objectify events and experiences and to deal with abstract issues.[216] It also probably lessens their ability to perceive social relations as governed by general rules and to understand the relevance of legal rights and duties. Furthermore, the indications are that the poor are less likely to know the rules governing court procedures, and are less likely to understand what they have observed in court.[217]

The narrow world of the poor also restricts their knowledge of opportunities provided in the law,[218] and limits familiarity with institutions and functionaries that could be of assistance in asserting and protecting legal rights. Studies have

216. As the sociologist C.C. North has put it, isolation from heterogeneous environments, characteristic of low status, operates to "limit the sources of information, to retard the development of efficiency in judgment and reasoning abilities, and to confine the attention to more trivial interests in life" S. LIPSET, POLITICAL MAN 120 (1960).

The difficulty of the poor in grasping abstractions is noted by lawyers who occasionally represent lower class persons. One lawyer, for example, gave us the following illustration:

> Before an Industrial Accident Commission hearing I try to alert the injured worker to the possibility that the insurance company has taken highly selective motion pictures of his recent behavior and suggest that he should very carefully consider his answers to questions concerning specific acts. I'll say, "opposing counsel may ask if you have mowed the lawn recently. And this probably means the insurance company has pictures of you mowing the lawn. So watch out for that kind of question. Tell them the truth." Now if counsel does ask my client if he mowed the lawn recently, the client will catch on and do what I told him. But if the lawyer asks him if he changed a tire recently, the client would not draw the analogy that this, too, is a specific act. He will probably answer "no" because not being able to change a tire is indicative of his disabled condition. And then they produce the movies.

Drawn from our field notes.

217. Respondents in a representative sample of 1,000 Texas adults were asked if they understood most of the court proceedings the last time they observed a trial. Forty-four per cent of persons with less than a high school education, compared to 15 per cent of those with a college education, said that there was much they did not understand when last in court. J. Belden, "What Texans Think of Lawyers" 43, unpublished manuscript, 1952. In a study of a mid-western community it was shown that middle class respondents were more likely to know "how many jurors must agree to reach a verdict." See A. BARTON & S. MENDLOVITZ, "THE COURT AND THE COMMUNITY: A STUDY OF CONTACTS, COMMUNICATIONS, AND OPINIONS REGARDING A SPECIALIZED LEGAL INSTITUTION" (Unpublished manuscript, 1956). The study was based on interviews with a probability sample of 102 adults in a midwestern city of about 120,000 people.

218. A Los Angeles study shows that almost half of 542 persons currently unemployed had never heard of "the Government retraining programs, night courses, or other programs to give more training to people." It was noted, however, that: "in response to an earlier question, about four-fifths of this same sampling had indicated an interest in retraining." See HARD-CORE UNEMPLOYMENT AND POVERTY IN LOS ANGELES 133, 217 (1965).

shown that low-income persons are less likely to be acquainted with lawyers and court personnel than are persons with high incomes.[219] Moreover, although free or low-cost legal services are sometimes available to them, a large proportion of low-income persons are apparently unaware of the existence of such services.[220]

The significance of a restricted environment for limiting awareness of the availability of legal help is indicated in Caplovitz' study of low-income consumers. He found that the more isolated and particularistic their social relations the less likely his respondents were to know where to go for help if they were being cheated by a merchant. Thus: (1) The newest group of migrants, the Puerto Ricans, were less well informed than Negroes and whites about where to get help;[221] (2) Those who had experience with "downtown" stores had less difficulty in naming sources

---

219. According to a Texas survey, 35 per cent of respondents of low socio-economic status did not know a lawyer in their community, compared to 18 per cent of those of upper- and upper-middle socioeconomic status. J. Belden, *supra* note 217, at 18. And a study of court contacts in a midwestern community shows that 52 per cent of respondents from business households and 53 per cent of those from white-collar households knew two or more court professionals (judges, lawyers or court employees), compared to only 12 per cent of semi-skilled and unskilled workers. A. Barton & S. Mendlovitz, *op. cit. supra* note 217.

It can be argued that the relationship between class and familiarity with lawyers is a function of the fact that lawyers belong to the middle and upper classes — not that classes differ in the breadth of their worlds. By either interpretation, however, it is clear that fewer of the poor than the rich have easy access to persons who can facilitate their use of the legal system.

220. An Iowa survey reports that 81 per cent of a quota sample of 234 low-income respondents have no knowledge of where free or low-cost legal services may be obtained. IOWA STATE BAR ASSN., LAY OPINION OF IOWA LAWYERS, COURTS AND LAWS 34 (1949). Whether this is due to lack of knowledge or lack of such services is perhaps an open question, although the Iowa survey treats it as the former noting: "While most lawyers provide such services on a personal basis, the extent of their contributions is not recognized." A California survey reports that about one-third of 582 lower-income respondents either believe free legal services are unobtainable or do not know where they can be found. LORD & THOMAS, PUBLIC OPINION POLL FOR THE STATE OF CALIFORNIA CODE 54 (1940). Koos found that almost one-half of his working class sample in Rochester, New York, had no idea or only a vague idea of the existence of a Legal Aid Society office in that city — even though Rochester was chosen for special study because it "has a Legal Aid Society which is efficient and has been in existence long enough to have become well-known in the community." E. Koos, THE FAMILY AND THE LAW 10 (1949).

221. Only 24% of the Puerto Ricans had some idea of where to get help, compared with 50% of the Negroes and 41% of the whites. Caplovitz notes: "As the newest immigrants, Puerto Ricans may be too insecure or too intimidated to find out what they can do about their problems. Or perhaps their friends and acquaintances are of little help, for they, too, do not know where to turn." D. Caplovitz, *op. cit. supra* note 180, at 177.

of help than those who shopped exclusively in the neighborhood;[222] (3) Knowledge of sources of help increased with the formal education of the household head, and this was true for each ethnic group.[223]

POWERLESSNESS

The poor tend to be at the bottom of all power structures; they are without resources. There can be little doubt that this is a major handicap to their using the legal system.

Lack of financial resources clearly contributes to the infrequent use of attorneys by the poor. Thus, it has been shown that the lower the respondent's class, the more likely he is to mention "price" or "expense" as a reason for not consulting lawyers.[224, 225] Even when a lawyer is retained, lack of financial resources makes it difficult to use the legal system in an effective manner. The "ordinary" troubles of life — illness, injury, death, loss of a job — make extraordinary demands on the poor; their resources are quickly exhausted. Lawyers who deal with poor persons in industrial accident and personal injury cases (where there is a contingent fee) tell us that poor clients often exert strong pressure to "settle out" so that they can pay their bills and have "something extra" to live on. Furthermore, in our society (and in many others) to be without financial resources is interpreted as a sign of general inadequacy, sapping belief in one's power of self-assertion.

The powerlessness of the poor is also revealed in their lack of control over the terms and conditions of their market relationships. They come to the bargaining table ignorant of their rights and powerless to enforce them; they are dependent on the goodwill and integrity of other parties, and are vulnerable to exploitation. When

---

222. Of those classified as having broad shopping scope 56% knew of a source for help compared with 24% of those with a narrow shopping scope. *Id.* at 176.

223. Sixty-six per cent of respondents from families in which the household head had a high school degree knew of a source for help, compared with 21% of those from families in which the household head had only an elementary school education. *Id.*

224. For example, Koos asked "working class" and "middle class" respondents to indicate if they had experienced any of 30 problems frequently serviced by lawyers; he then asked them to say why they had not consulted a lawyer (if they had not). About 48 per cent of the working class respondents said they were unable to afford the fees; an additional 6 per cent said they would not "take charity." Twelve per cent of middle class respondents said they were unable to afford the fees; none mentioned charity. E. Koos, *op. cit. supra* note 220.

225. A California survey shows that 54 per cent of "lower class" and 31 per cent of "upper class" respondents said "price" or "expense" was the reason they would not seek legal advice from a lawyer. Lord & Thomas, *op. cit. supra* note 220.

the poor deal with landlords, merchants, employers or creditors, they deal from a position of weakness, and they are usually afraid to press claims or grievances for fear of reprisal. They fear eviction if they complain about housing code violations; they fear denial of future credit if they complain about "shady" sales practices; they fear loss of job if they press a wage or accident claim against an employer.

Their powerlessness is also evident in their relations with government agencies. Thus, Coser argues:

> The poor, when receiving assistance, are assigned a low and degraded status by virtue of a determination that they cannot themselves contribute to society. Their inability to contribute in turn degrades them to the condition of unilateral receivers.[226]

The poor are thus forced into a position of

> "unquestioning acceptance, of an expert's dictation of what is 'good for the client,' and of an administrator's unchecked and unreviewable authority to terminate assistance. That power defines a status of subserviency and evokes fear, resentment and resignation on the part of the donee."[227]

Government by threat and fear tends to become a substitute for governance by law, and the poor accordingly become skeptical of the possibility of holding authorities accountable — they have little confidence in the efficacy of invoking the law to secure their interests.

ORGANIZATIONAL PARTICIPATION

Membership in organizations can play a crucial role in developing and sustaining legal competence. Organizations can increase members' awareness of their legal rights and obligations, promote a sense of security in asserting claims and imbue members with a concern for the broader (collective) implications of their grievances and with a sense of duty to assert rights where group interests are at stake. There are also more direct ways in which organizations can help promote effective use of the legal system. They can lobby before a legislative or an administrative body, file an *amicus curiae* brief before an appellate tribunal, initiate legal proceedings — and provide the necessary continuity and resources for the effective processing of legal actions.[228] Organizations may also facilitate the use of private attorneys: by reducing the cost of legal services (e.g., through a group insurance

---

226. L. Coser, *The Sociology of Poverty*, 13 SOCIAL PROBLEMS 141, 147 (1965).

227. E. Cahn & J. Cahn, *supra* note 179, at 1321-22.

228. Clement E. Vose, *Litigation as a Form of Pressure Group Activity*, 319 ANNALS 22 (Sept. 1958).

plan) or by recommending particular lawyers to their members and certifying their competence and integrity.

One of the principal characteristics of the poor, however, is their very low rate of organizational participation.[229] The poor fail to participate in organizations because they see little relation between their own interests and purposes of the group, and because they find it hard to believe they could in any way influence the attainment of organizational goals.

The poor are unlikely to be members of political organizations or to participate in other forms of political activity. Herbert Gans has described the inability of Boston's poor "West-enders" to block urban redevelopment plans to which they "were almost unanimously opposed."[230] He observes: "They could not break out of the[ir] peer group society and organize in common cause."[231] Robert Lane has summarized a number of studies showing the relation between low economic status and low political participation.[232] Almond and Verba have shown that this relation holds for the five countries they studied.[233]

The history of trade union and civil rights movements suggests the very great importance of organized political action for implementing legal competence, particularly among those groups that tend to be most apathetic.[234] A demonstration of collective power may instill a sense of common cause and increase confidence in the efficacy of action and one's ability to challenge and criticize authority. This mobilization of consensus around issues and interests of particular relevance to certain groups may also increase the capacity of these groups to develop into effective constituencies of legal institutions, and could provide a more favorable climate for

---

229. A. Cohen & H. Hodges, *supra* note 213, at 315. See also G. Knupfer, *Portrait of the Underdog,* in CLASS, STATUS AND POWER: A READER IN SOCIAL STRATIFICATION 256, 258, 262 (R. Bendix & S. Lipset eds. 1953); J. KAHL, THE AMERICAN CLASS STRUCTURE 147 (1957); M. HARRINGTON, THE OTHER AMERICA 26-27 (1964); D. Caplovitz, *op. cit. supra* note 180, at 133 where he notes "For the sample as a whole, and within each social group, the more solvent families more often belong to voluntary associations."

230. H. GANS, THE URBAN VILLAGERS 289 (1962).

231. *Id.* at 296.

232. R. LANE, POLITICAL LIFE pts. II & IV, 16 (1965).

233. See G. Almond & S. Verba, *op. cit. supra* note 202, at 210 fig. 3. The countries were the United States, Great Britain, Germany, Italy and Mexico.

234. The Negro Church has played a crucial role in fostering Negro participation in the civil rights movement. By assuming this political function the church has given the movement a valuable organizational base.

asserting claims of right within the adjudicative process. Thus, a referendum, a boycott, or even a riot, may compel authorities to establish more effective means for considering and responding to legal grievances. Political action, however, need not engender a commitment to using *legal* channels for righting wrongs. Indeed, the relation between political and legal competence and the conditions under which the one leads to the other should be a central research question that may be fruitfully explored among the poor. It is clear that political action may have legal effect. At the same time participation in the legal process may be a crucial component of the citizen role. Meaningful enfranchisement, it has been contended, encompasses active involvement "in all organs of government — both public and private — where law is made."[235]

EXPERIENCE WITH THE LEGAL SYSTEM

Taking legal action rests, in part, on the expectation that it will result in a net gain, that it will be worth the effort. The expectation of effectiveness is, in turn, related to one's previous experience, including experience with the legal system.[236]

The life situation of the poor generally works against the expectation that present effort will lead to future reward. Rather it tends to support the conviction that purposive effort is usually futile, that misfortune is the product of fate or other forces over which the individual has no effective control. This apathetic stance reflects in part the shortened "time span of expectations" of the poor, their inability to plan for the future, to "perceive the complex possibilities and consequences of action." As Lipset has noted: "From early childhood, [the lower-class person] has sought immediate gratification, rather than engage in activities that might have long-term rewards. The logic of both his adult employment and his family situation reinforces this limited time perspective."[237]

The poor man's conviction of the futility of purposive effort is also reinforced by the character of his experience with the legal system. His encounters with the law typically occur with police, probation officers, process servers and welfare workers, involving, therefore, direct contact with those agents of the law who seek to control,

235. E. Cahn & J. Cahn, *The War on Poverty: A Civilian Perspective*, 73 YALE L.J. 1317, 1334 (1964).

236. For example, a recent study of accident victims in New York City found that if the victim had obtained a money recovery in a previous accident he was more likely to make some effort to recover for his loss in the case at hand than if he had never been in a previous accident; those who failed to recover in the previous accident were least likely to make an effort to recover now. See J. Carlin, *op. cit. supra* note 206.

237. S. Lipset, *op. cit. supra* note 216, at 415.

if not punish him. This leads to a negative if not openly antagonistic attitude toward the legal system, to a conception of the law as something that works against his interests, as a source of deprivation and abuse, rather than as a viable or effective resource for vindicating rights. As Robert Kennedy has observed: "The poor man looks upon the law as an enemy, not as a friend. For him the law is always taking something away."[238] The police, in particular, are often perceived by the poor as brutal, greedy and corrupt.[239]

In dealings with court and agency officials the poor are often treated with indifference or in a patronizing or humiliating manner. Thus, in order to demonstrate their eligibility to receive welfare benefits they are frequently subjected to what has been termed a "degradation ceremony."[240]

The experience of the poor in the courts is strongly affected by the fact that

---

238. E. Cahn & J. Cahn, *supra* note 235, at 1337 no. 27.

239. See L. Zeitz, *supra* note 208, at 25, where he concludes: "The police are seen (by lower-class Negroes), at least in their active roles, as antipathetic (at best) to (their interests). . . . Mention of the police brought forth a deluge of complaints ranging from callousness and apathy through brutality and extortions."

In the recent report on the Watts riot it was noted:

> "Police brutality" has been the recurring charge (of Negroes appearing before the Commission as witnesses). One witness after another has recounted instances in which, in their opinion, the police have used excessive force or have been disrespectful and abusive in their language or manner. . . . The reasons for the feeling that law enforcement officers are the enemy of the Negro are manifold and it is well to reflect on them. . . . In each of the 1964 riots, "police brutality" was an issue, as it has been here.

THE GOVERNOR'S COMMISSION ON THE LOS ANGELES RIOTS, VIOLENCE IN THE CITY — AN END OR A BEGINNING 27, 28, 29 (1965).

240. See H. Garfinkel, *Conditions of Successful Degradation Ceremonies*, 61 AM. J. Soc. 420 (1956). As the Moreland Commission observes with respect to New York State:

> An applicant becomes eligible for assistance when he exhausts his money, gives a lien on his property to the welfare department, turns in the license plates of his car and takes legal action against his legally responsible relatives. When he is stripped of all material resources, when he "proves" his dependency, then only is he eligible. Welfare policies tend to cast the recipient in the role of the propertyless shiftless pauper. This implies he is incompetent and inadequate to meet the demands of competitive life. He is then regarded as if he had little or no feelings, aspirations or normal sensibilities. This process of proving and maintaining eligibilty in combination with the literal adherence to regulations and procedures tends to produce a self-perpetuating system of dependency and dehumanization.

REPORT TO THE MORELAND COMMISSION ON THE WELFARE FINDINGS OF THE PUBLIC ASSISTANCE PROGRAM AND OPERATIONS OF THE STATE OF NEW YORK 78 (1962).

they are typically defendants, not plaintiffs, and as *poor* defendants they find themselves in a doubly disadvantaged position. With reference to landlord-tenant disputes it has been observed:

> Because litigation generally occurs with the tenant on the defensive, there is an understandable temptation for an over-worked judge to suppose that the tenant, like many others who appear before him, is desirous primarily of a chance to welch on his rent . . . it is easier to picture a tenant as a responsible citizen if he seeks a court order to improve his building than if he is hauled into court for nonpayment of rent.[241]

The implication is that a tenant's defense alleging landlord malfeasance is suspect specifically because it is a *defense*. "Over-worked" judges are tempted to presume guilt and to rule accordingly.

The likelihood of a plaintiff's verdict is increased by the fact that the poor defendant typically stands alone, without counsel, without resources, often facing overwhelming odds. His opponents are generally not other individuals but organizations — business firms, or agencies of government. Even in matters that ostensibly involve private individuals, such as domestic relations disputes, government is likely to be an interested party because the poor are frequently wards of the state. Thus, in non-support cases poor husbands and fathers are likely to be opposed by welfare agents, probation officers and district attorneys.

In their more infrequent role as plaintiffs the poor may also have unrewarding experiences, because the stakes involved are usually too small for the legal system to give their problems careful attention, and because their problems are often not amenable to solution by conventional legal process.

The poor person's perception of the legal system as indifferent if not hostile to his interests is reinforced by the meager representation of the poor among those who make and administer the law. Only rarely do poor persons become judges or administrators, and they are seldom elected to legislative bodies. At best they may serve in advisory capacities, with little likelihood that their views will be given more than token recognition. Moreover, the few who make it into more important positions of power are not necessarily sympathetic to the interests of the poor — they may be "bought out" by the establishment. The social distance of the poor from those in power is one more factor contributing to their negative ex-

---

241. J. Levi, "The Legal Needs of the Poor: Problems Relating to Real Property," p. 10, paper read at the National Conference on Law and Poverty, Washington, D.C., June 23-25, 1965.

perience with the legal system, discouraging them from using the law to further their interests.

That the poor man's encounters with the law lead to alienation from the legal system is strongly indicated in the relation between prior court contact and the willingness of accident victims to take some action to recover for their losses.[242] The more often respondents had come into contact with the courts, the *less* likely they were to take action — and this was especially true of lower class respondents.

Where there is some evidence of success in pursuing legal channels, as in the case of civil rights legislation and Supreme Court decisions prohibiting discrimination in education, a more favorable attitude emerges. Thus, when respondents in the New Jersey study were asked: "What is the best way for Negroes to get their civil rights?" approximately one-third suggested strengthening the law we now have and one-fourth recommended enactment of new laws.[243] Moreover, the "Newsweek poll" of Negro attitudes toward civil rights shows a highly favorable evaluation of the Supreme Court as an institution for the implementation of Negro rights. Respondents were given "a list of different people and groups that are run by white people" and asked whether each had been more helpful or more harmful to Negro rights. In evaluating the Supreme Court, 85% of the respondents said "more helpful"; only one institution, the Kennedy Administration, received a higher proportion of favorable responses.[244]

CONCLUSION

In this section of the paper, we have considered some of the features of the life-situation of the poor that appear to contribute to their legal incompetence. Without pretending to be exhaustive we have suggested that legal competence depends on a sense of oneself as a bearer of rights and of the legal system as a resource for developing and implementing these rights. We have suggested that their narrow world, powerlessness, lack of organizational participation and negative legal experience tend to give the poor a conception of themselves and the legal system that is incompatible with effective use of the law.

Broadly speaking there would seem to be two ways to deal with the relative incompetence of the poor.[245]

---

242. J. Carlin, *op. cit. supra* note 206.
243. L. Zeitz, *supra* note 208, at 301.
244. W. Brink & L. Harris, *op. cit. supra* note 211, at 234.
245. See L. Zeitz, *supra* note 208, at 310.

First, an effort might be made to increase their competence. Any changes that would enhance the accessibility of legal remedies would serve this function, e.g., providing free, localized legal service. Reducing the dependence of the poor on those who can or do deny them their rights would also make them more competent, e.g., encouraging the organization of persons receiving public assistance.

Second, the legal system might be changed in ways that would make legal competence less relevant. Anti-discrimination agencies might be empowered and encouraged to initiate action in the absence of complaints.[246] Judges and administrators might be given greater powers to interpret and articulate the interests of the poor, as apparently happens to some extent in the juvenile court and perhaps other settings as well. And checks might be built into the system that do not depend on the initiative of parties or their resources. On the criminal side the automatic appeal in capital cases is an illustration of this. On the civil side, such checks might be provided through an Ombudsman.[247]

It is important to suggest, however, that it is difficult to see how the legal system could totally do away with the need for competence of parties and still provide justice. Moreover, reliance on alternative methods for controlling official discretion would seem to lead to a problem of infinite regress: the problem of who governs the governors. Perhaps all that would be accomplished in the long run would be to relocate the competence problem. Matters now settled in court or before administrative tribunals might be settled before the legislature or the executive; but the task of bringing influence to bear on official decision makers would remain a necessity.

These considerations suggest the need for a combination of strategies. Justice in a society such as ours, a society marked by wide differences in wealth, power and their accompaniments, would seem to require that the legal system not be blind to differences in legal competence; that instead it be moved to compensate for these differences. In selecting the form of compensation, however, those who operate the system should be aware of the fact that although certain changes may contribute to the development of the legal competence of parties, others may well tend to reinforce incompetence.

---

246. *Ibid.*

247. See K. D. Davis, *Ombudsmen in America: Officers to Criticize Administrative Actions,* 109 U. PA. L. REV. 1057 (1961). Also see R. Cloward & R. Elman, *Poverty, Injustice and the Welfare State: An Ombudsman for the Poor?,* 202 THE NATION 230 (February 28, 1966).

SUMMARY AND CONCLUSION

Our examination of issues in the area of civil justice and the poor has necessarily been based on very limited data, much of it open to serious question. In this concluding section we shall indicate certain areas in which further investigation would be particularly useful.

We have suggested that the poor no less than the rich have legal problems, that they are even more likely than the rich to suffer injustices resulting from the operation of our economic and governmental systems. We have said that many of the abuses experienced by the poor arise from institutionalized practices, and that these collective problems are often unaffected by, if not exacerbated by, traditional legal controls. In fact, however, we know very little about the range or incidence of injustices experienced by individuals in different segments of the society. In the consumer area we need systematic studies of the incidence of missed payments on installment contracts, the frequency with which missed payments result in repossession or garnishment and the extent to which garnishment leads to loss of job. Repossessions are said to be made in illegal ways, deficiency judgments granted without due notice to the debtor and wage attachments applied to larger portions of the debtor's wages than legally justified. How common are these practices, and what are the conditions that give rise to and sustain them? The public sphere, too, contributes its share of important legal problems, probably an increasing share. What is the experience of those who must deal with welfare and unemployment insurance agencies, county hospitals, public housing authorities? What kinds of abuses are routinely met in these situations? How are they dealt with?

We are interested not only in a description of injustices and their incidence in different social classes. Research is also required to illuminate the character of the institutional settings in which injustices arise, the various pressures leading to the initiation and establishment of abusive practices and the capacity of firms and agencies for institutionalizing procedures that might prevent or restrict such practices.

LAW

The law is, above all, a means of creating and protecting rights. We must inquire more fully into the extent to which it performs this essential function for the poor. For example, to what extent do potential recipients of public assistance have recourse through law when they are denied assistance, or when benefits are reduced, or are less than the recipient is entitled to? To the extent that the law provides determinate criteria for eligibility decisions and regular procedures for challenging these decisions, the benefit takes on the character of a "right." To the extent that the criteria are vague — or to the extent that the law fails to require public assistance administrators to make their criteria known — the benefit remains "a privilege." We know something of the conditions under which "privileges" are transformed into "rights" — this has happened, for example, to benefits for the aged.[248] More inquiry is needed.

But this is not the only issue. We must also inquire into the *character* of the rights which may be accorded by law. An important fact about assistance is that many persons who are apparently qualified *do not enter a claim*. There are a number of reasons for this, some of which have been considered in our discussion of "legal competence." One of the reasons is that many people apparently consider a claim for public assistance to be an admission of "failure"; given current definitions it seems to connote that one is less than whole. Is there any alternative? It is worth noting that others receive public benefits (*e.g.*, subsidies) without suffering the degradation allegedly experienced by those on "public assistance." We should inquire more closely into the consequences of transforming "assistance" into a "pension."[249] Study of this process among the aged might provide a useful beginning. A simple change of *terms* — the invention of euphemisms for public assistance or relief investigation, for example — is not enough. What is needed is the conviction, which can be expressed in law, that those receiving benefits have given something in the past for which they are now being remunerated, or that they are giving something now.

Research is obviously required to document areas of inequality in the law (*de facto* as well as *de jure*), and to explore criteria for determining the nature and extent of inequality. Studies should also be directed at what is perhaps a more fundamental issue: what are the potential resources within existing areas of law for promoting the interests and aspirations of the poor and for insuring conformity of official action to the rule of law?

ADMINISTRATION OF JUSTICE

We have suggested that justice is administered in many settings. One of the principal problems, regardless of setting, is that agencies administering justice tend

---

248. See F. PINNER, P. JACOBS & P. SELZNICK, OLD AGE AND POLITICAL BEHAVIOR: A CASE STUDY (1959).

249. A similar recommendation was proposed many years ago by Ludwig Bendix in L. Bendix, *Richter, Rechtsanwälte und Arbeitsgerichte*, 2 Die Justiz 188-89 (1926).

to be large-scale organizations faced with the task of processing an ever increasing volume of cases. To what extent is it possible to preserve minimal standards of fairness within a framework of mass-production justice? Can we provide decent justice at low cost?

The tendency to conceive of treatment and rehabilitation as the primary objectives of tribunals and agencies serving the poor may also weaken the adjudicative process. How extensive is this development; what are the conditions that sustain it; and to what extent are these newer goals in fact realizable? More important, to what extent is this development necessarily inconsistent with the preservation of certain standards of procedural fairness?

Study of agencies applying law to the poor reveals the difficulties of maintaining a commitment to serving the needs and interests of poor constituents. Welfare agencies, for example, have apparently been more zealous to see that those *not* entitled to benefits did not receive them than they have been to insure that those entitled did in fact receive them. The history of the development of internal controls within public assistance agencies remains to be written. When it is written it will probably show that controls developed first to see that assistance officials did not extend benefits to the ineligible and to prevent fraud on the part of applicants. Lately, it appears that controls are developing which at least permit the agency to rectify another sort of administrative error — the denial of benefits to those entitled to them. This implies, of course, that those who are entitled apply for benefits. We know that many do not. To date there appears to be little activity on the part of agencies to see that those entitled to benefits *do* apply.

Controlling administrative behavior is ordinarily taken to mean controlling "arbitrariness." This is crucially important. But the term itself requires more analysis than it has received to date. To do nothing is also a form of official arbitrariness. When this occurs on a mass scale — as it apparently has in public assistance — it is not obvious that traditional forms of litigation will serve to change the situation.

The problem we have discussed here applies beyond public assistance; in many ways it is the same problem confronted by Blumrosen in his study of the New Jersey Civil Rights Division — moving public agencies to positive action.[250] Is this a matter that is appropriately dealt with through adjudication? Or, are administrative or legislative reforms called for? This is clearly an area requiring careful and serious study.

---

250. A. Blumrosen, *op cit. supra* note 138.

It should be noted that "passivity" in the above sense is very much related to the "character of rights" problem discussed earlier. Of principal concern here is the way in which the character of rights affects the agencies rather than the clients. When the right is, say, a scientific scholarship, one would expect the agency to engage in a search for those who might be entitled to it. How can we achieve a definition of public assistance that will convey a similarly positive stance to the administrators? It may be difficult to convince the public that failure to provide support for the destitute is against the public good.

Finally, we should not overlook the obvious need for sociological studies of the adjudicative process within various court and agency settings, studies of the judiciary and studies of the "clients" or "constituents" of legal agencies.

LEGAL PROFESSION

A major issue in the area of law and poverty concerns the extension of legal representation to the poor. What are the problems encountered in the effort to expand legal services and to develop new organizational forms for the provision of such services? What problems are raised as we move away from the more traditional, individualized forms of representation, with a direct, personal relation between lawyer and client, to group or collective representation? Not the least of these problems is a potential conflict between the needs and demands of particular clients and the goals and interests of the group. Moreover, with a weakening of the traditional lawyer-client relation attorneys may be less inclined to follow the dictates of the client than to follow their own ideas as to what is in the best interests of the client. As a result, a form of paternalism may tend to replace commitment to legal advocacy.

The tendency for legal institutions, particularly those concerned with the poor, to become large-scale organizations, extends not only to courts and tribunals but to agencies providing legal services as well. Thus, the analogue to mass-production justice for the poor may be the development of mass-production techniques in the provision of legal services. The implications of this development for the character and quality of legal services, and for the integrity of the adjudicative process should be a major area of research.

Although there appears to be considerable variation by social class in the quality and availability of legal services the data on which such conclusions are based are far from satisfactory. In addition to further studies of legal services provided by private attorneys we need to know a great deal more about the operation of Legal

Aid, various forms of group legal service (as developed by trade unions, legal defense organizations such as the NAACP, and the armed services), and of course the new federally financed legal service programs.

LEGAL COMPETENCE

The poor are apparently most deficient in legal competence. Such data as we have examined indicate that the poor do not actively seek to further their interests through the legal system and that they lack the capacity to take effective legal action. More specifically, the data suggest that: (1) the use of lawyers and courts is directly correlated with socio-economic status, and (2) the poor are unlikely to use the legal system in situations in which one might expect them to do so. Although existing studies show a reasonable consistency in their main findings, they usually leave much to be desired in terms of sample size and sophistication of research design and analysis.

The basic question to be explored is this: What does it mean to be an effective participant in the legal order? This calls for study of the capacity not only to use existing instrumentalities of the law to protect and implement rights, but to increase the availability and responsiveness of legal institutions. What special qualities are required of individuals and groups in order to move the legal system? What are the social conditions that support and undermine these qualities? We have suggested some of the ways in which the conditions of poverty may tend to undermine legal competence; there are few studies, however, which seek explicitly to explore these relationships. Such research might also examine how experience with the legal system affects legal competence. To what extent do encounters with the law lead to alienation from the legal system? For what groups? Under what conditions?

We are also led to inquire into the interplay between legal and political competence: What distinguishes one from the other? In what ways does political action contribute to legal competence? Under what conditions does it tend to weaken legal competence? What are the political implications of legal action?

Finally, we need to learn more about the significance of legal competence for enhancing the quality of the legal system. To what extent are there meaningful substitutes for the legal competence of the governed, and what are the consequences of adopting such substitutes?